O9-BUD-712

ca was split

—not

en North

uth...

WHAT
TRUTH
SOUNDS
LIKE

Also by Michael Eric Dyson
and available from St. Martin's Press

Tears We Cannot Stop:
A Sermon to White America

WHAT
TRUTH
SOUNDS
LIKE

ROBERT F. KENNEDY,
JAMES BALDWIN, AND OUR
UNFINISHED CONVERSATION
ABOUT RACE IN AMERICA

MICHAEL
ERIC
DYSON

ST. MARTIN'S PRESS ☰ NEW YORK

WHAT TRUTH SOUNDS LIKE. Copyright © 2018 by Michael Eric Dyson. All rights reserved. Printed in the United States of America. For information, address St. Martin's Press, 175 Fifth Avenue, New York, NY 10010.

Small portions of my work that appeared in the *New York Times* are adopted here in different form in "Politicians" and "Activists 1"; parts of my "The Ghosts of Cornel West" and "Yes She Can" pieces for the *New Republic* have been adapted and incorporated into "The Intellectuals" and "The Activists 1."

www.stmartins.com

Library of Congress Cataloging-in-Publication Data is available upon request.

ISBN 978-1-250-19941-6 (hardcover)
ISBN 978-1-250-19942-3 (ebook)

Our books may be purchased in bulk for promotional, educational, or business use. Please contact your local bookseller or the Macmillan Corporate and Premium Sales Department at 1-800-221-7945, extension 5442, or by email at MacmillanSpecialMarkets@macmillan.com.

First Edition: June 2018

10 9 8 7 6 5 4 3 2 1

To Crystal McCrary and Ray McGuire

Dear Friends

Living Embodiments of Black America's

Grace and Genius

Contents

WHAT
TRUTH
SOUNDS
LIKE

THE MARTYRS

The blood of martyrs soaks the soil of American society. The life given to us by the deaths of a few has altered the course of history and strengthened the heartbeat of justice in our breasts. The willingness to surrender one's life for a righteous cause doesn't come easy. Neither does it keep the depraved men who kill our heroes from believing they are driven by destiny or divinity. But the sacrifice of extraordinary figures has given us a firmer grasp of truth and democracy than their killers ever imagined. John Wilkes Booth may have wished to stop the liberation of enslaved blacks when he murdered Abraham Lincoln, but he strengthened their cause with his fatal shot.

In the nineteen sixties, the deaths of three men changed America and caused us to reckon anew with our ideals. John F. Kennedy made us hope that American ingenuity would triumph over ignorance, that science would defeat superstition. His youthful effort to tame our cynicism ended tragically in 1963 on a dark day in Dallas. His brother Robert met a similar fate just five years later. Robert had emerged from his brother's shadow to lay claim to a reviving sense of national purpose: to slay the dragons of poverty and to vanquish the demons of insincerity. Between their assassinations was lodged the death of a man who was arguably greater than them both. He held no office nor did he enjoy the privileges of white skin. He sought to cure the American soul of its bigotry against a black people it had snatched from a far continent, a black people that the nation had, for corrupt purposes, fettered in its twisted white imagination. Martin Luther King, Jr., crushed the facade of American decency and called on us to revisit our neglected moral ambition, preaching the gospel of love in a time of withering hate.

Fifty years ago, on April 9, 1968, at 10:30 a.m., 1,300 people filed into Ebenezer Baptist Church in Atlanta for the private funeral of a man who, like his father before him, had once served as its pastor: the Reverend Martin Luther King, Jr. Attendees included Thurgood Marshall, Wilt Chamberlain, Marlon Brando, Dizzy Gillespie, Stokely Carmichael, and Richard Nixon, who was then running for president. The sitting president, Lyndon Baines Johnson, did not come because he didn't want to drape the service in the controversy of the Vietnam War, a cause to which he had devoted significant resources. The choir, 160 strong, sang sorrowful hymns. King's dear friend and gospel legend Mahalia Jackson delivered a plaintive accounting of the fallen leader's favorite hymn, "Take My Hand, Precious Lord." Ralph David Abernathy, cofounder of the Southern Christian Leadership Conference and a man whom King described as "the best friend I have in the world," officiated.[1] A lone singer performed a devastating rendition of "My Heavenly Father Watches Over Me."

But the most memorable speaker that morning—a haunting baritone piped out of tinny speakers that left his four children startled—was King himself. "If any of you are around when I have to meet my day, I don't want a long funeral," King pleaded posthumously in a recording from his "Drum Major Instinct" sermon given two months earlier and played at the behest of his widow, Coretta. He didn't get his wish: The service lasted two hours, followed by a public, nationally broadcast funeral held that afternoon at King's alma mater, Morehouse College.

As a nine-year-old kid in the Detroit ghetto, I was drawn to the television screen to view the funeral. I was just beginning to understand my blackness, just learning that it existed, that it was essential in a world where whiteness loomed as an unknowable force. I had never gone to school with white kids, had rarely even interacted with white folk outside of the neighborhood business owners for whom my father, and eventually I, worked. I didn't know what they liked or how they thought of the world, how they handled their disappointments or whether they, like us, laughed at misery to keep from crying. I was only starting to sense that white folk may have feared us as much as they didn't like us; it seemed vaguely tied to how we refused to bow in the face of suffering and how, despite their doing the worst they could imagine doing to us, we refused to give in.

With King's death, the whiteness that had been shapeless suddenly lunged forward. When King was killed, I felt vulnerable; all that made sense no longer held in place, and it appeared that the cosmos had gotten drunk on its insufficiency, teetered off course, and hurtled madly toward oblivion. How else could it be? Martin Luther King, Jr., was put down like a mangy dog. His breathing and being were seen as such an offense that they had to be stopped at all costs. I was frightened for months. He had been murdered on a balcony, and I could no longer easily wash my hands in our bathroom, which opened onto an upstairs balcony, without fearing that whiteness would kill me too.

Perhaps that was why I paid such close attention to his funeral; I was in search of unspoken solace, of comfort that could only come if I could discern in his services some logic, some possible clue, for why he had to perish, some explanation that might, I felt too guilty to admit, spare me his same fate. My father thought it was all morbid. He eventually sent me outside to play, but not before I eagerly drank in the mournful cadences of the folk gathered at King's public service. They surely grieved for King and his valiant family, and, yes, for themselves. But their grief had become a ritual that was all too familiar when a leader or an ordinary soul had been silenced by white rage; and by then our rituals could barely contain moments like this, moments for which we had no words.

Yet any writer must have words, especially if he is a witness, even a prophet, though not quite as piercing as the one who lay in his grave.

Make no mistake, James Baldwin had words. He shared with that fallen soul a style forged in the black pulpit. Jimmy attended the funeral too, having wrangled his way through the massive throng outside before he was hoisted atop a car and seated inside the sanctuary. In "Malcolm and Martin," the essay he wrote four years after King's assassination, Baldwin recalled King's funeral—"the most real church service I've ever sat through in my life"—then grappled with the national undoing set loose by his death.[2]

I had just begun reading Baldwin at the time King was murdered. I inhaled his semiautobiographical *Go Tell It on the Mountain,* identifying with the main character, John Grimes, and his intense struggles with the church and the passionate effort to reconcile religion and rationality. Not long afterward I began sampling

Baldwin's legendary essays. Baldwin inspired me to read between the lines and beneath the surface, reading me into black manhood with the wise counsel and steady affection of a big brother or loving father.

By the time I got to his essay on Malcolm and Martin, I'd grown out of my racial innocence, a process that began with the '67 rebellion in Detroit. Just as police brutality vexes black life today, an act of police aggression sparked what was then the deadliest riot in the nation's history. We lived in the perilous shadow of relentless surveillance and intimidation by law enforcement. One night, at an illegal after-hours joint where black folk were celebrating the return of two Vietnam veterans to the Motor City, police hostility made it clear that it was often easier to survive the Viet Cong than the vicious cops. My fellow Detroiters had had enough of being pushed around and hammered with heedless agitation. The city exploded in fiery violence.

I already believed that America could only purge its hateful bigotry if it confronted its past with the same energy it embraced its founding fathers and celebrated the myth of American individualism. I had begun speaking in public at age twelve, and James Baldwin could always be relied on to inspire such an enterprise with his withering indictment of white innocence and his ceaseless effort to tell the truth.

Baldwin knew that America could only survive if it underwent an extraordinary social transformation—

equality for all, hatred for none—that echoed the most noble ideals set out by our founding fathers. (That is, when they set aside their blinding prejudice.) But he also knew that King's death, and Malcolm X's in 1965, were portents of the nation's refusal to acknowledge that the key to its salvation was held by those very people whom it had enslaved. The former quickly embraced pacifism; the latter was an advocate for black freedom at any cost. But the daily battles took a toll on both men, and their views had begun to converge—Malcolm mellowed; Martin grew more radical—so that, as Baldwin writes, "by the time each met his death there was practically no difference between them."[3] Not that the country much cared about the particulars; the American experiment had once again failed to trust that its redemption would come through black moral genius and paid the price for its disbelief.

America, Baldwin believed, was split in two—not between North and South but between the powerful and the disenfranchised. Racism, that scourge that beclouded our democracy, remained—remains—the nation's greatest peril. But the powerful maintained the status quo by sowing discord among the disenfranchised. Poor white folk, rather than uniting with their socioeconomically oppressed brothers and sisters against the rich, trained their ire on poor black folk. They channeled their anxieties into a vengeance against blackness.

In this way, Baldwin predicted the forces that would one day lead to the return of xenophobic white nationalism, to the rise of Donald Trump. But to say Baldwin was ahead of his time is to miss his point: America will always need a martyr, a prophet—a Malcolm, a Martin. The powerful will always seek to silence that prophet, trying to achieve the nation's redemption on the cheap—not through self-correction, but through crimson-stained violence that sacrifices the Other, whether black or brown or queer or immigrant. Fifty years after one lone prophet who didn't make it to forty gave up the ghost on a bland balcony in Memphis, King's legacy, and Baldwin's words, are as urgent as ever.

So too is the legacy of Robert F. Kennedy, who was at King's funeral and who would meet his own end less than two months later. When Robert Kennedy was assassinated, it left a far bigger impression on me than did the brutal death of his brother, President John F. Kennedy in 1963. I was too young to know how much black folk loved John Kennedy, though he sometimes dragged his feet on racial progress, equivocating on civil rights legislation. But by the time Robert Kennedy perished, I had a keener sense of how much his efforts to bring racial justice to the land resonated among black folk. Bobby Kennedy was the first white person I believed cared for black folk, and the sorrow and grief his death evoked in black America made me realize I wasn't alone.

Bobby Kennedy was widely viewed as a white man of means who was willing to lay it all on the line to help the vulnerable in our nation. As a politician, he seemed to spurn small talk for big ideas; he could be blunt, sometimes angry, in the pursuit of his goals, but he was willing to learn by listening. First as attorney general, then as a senator, and later as a presidential candidate, Bobby was eager to engage folk, to come face-to-face with people who might have interesting and helpful points of view.

Bobby's eagerness to engage occasionally got him more than he'd bargained for, and that was never truer than when he had an encounter that felt as if he had stepped onto a fast-moving train of rage and grief. When he invited James Baldwin to assemble an intimate gathering of friends to discuss race in May 1963, he had no idea that he was setting himself up for a colossal failure. He didn't anticipate the sober lesson ahead: even elite Negroes, no matter their station, feel the pain of their less fortunate brothers and sisters; they remain in touch with their people, and indeed, with their very humanity.

The meeting intrigues me because it teamed Bobby and Jimmy, and, though he was absent, Martin Luther King, Jr., as moral touchstone and racial reference. I heard over the years how explosive it was, how it brought together other folk I had admired, including Harry Belafonte. The gathering pitted an earnest if defensive white liberal against a raging phalanx of thinkers, activists, and entertainers who were out for blood. I've always wanted to read a book about that historic moment, and, more important, about its meaning for us today as we struggle with many of the same issues America confronted 50 years ago.

Each of the groups that participated in that bitter clash—the politicians, the artists, the intellectuals, the activists—is vital if we are to continue the conversation on race that began that day. Fifty-five years after Baldwin and Kennedy met and matched wits, we are in dire need of more talk, more insight, more wisdom, and, yes, more productive conflict, if we are to learn from our past in order to move forward in the present. Everything that hampered them hampers us; everything that hangs on the horizon of hope can be usefully exploited now, including the willingness to talk to one another across the crushing chasm of color. We desperately need to return to that room to wrestle our way to an uplifting resolution to seemingly intractable problems. And if hope led people, despite their differences, to that room more than 50 years ago, hope will still be our guide in continuing that conversation today.

THE MEETING

On Saturday morning, May 25, 1963, *The New York Times* trumpeted on its front page, in bold italics: "Robert Kennedy Consults Negroes Here About North."[1] The subtitle was set in smaller print so that a few of the notables who attended the meeting could be named. "James Baldwin, Lorraine Hansberry and Lena Horne Are Among Those Who Warn Him of 'Explosive Situation.'" The Gray Lady deemed the meeting important enough to give it pride of place above the fold. The article, penned by Layhmond Robinson, one of the first black reporters at the *Times,* disclosed in the lede that Kennedy "held a secret meeting . . . with a group of prominent Negroes to obtain their views on methods of combating segregation and discrimination in the North." According to Robinson, the group told RFK "that an 'explosive situation' had developed in race relations in the North that, potentially, was at least equal to the growing strife in the South." Perhaps one of the most interesting features of the article is that it noted the absence of leaders of civil rights groups and cited, instead, the presence of "well-known writers and other professional persons who have served as unofficial spokesmen for their race."

What made a meeting between a leading white politician and a group of prominent black artists, activists, and intellectuals worthy of a story on the front page of arguably the nation's most prestigious newspaper at the height of America's second civil war?

The year 1963 was a landmark in the struggle for black freedom. The Birmingham movement got underway in April and would eventually include the presence of women and especially children, turning the tide of events toward a resolution of lethal hostilities. It drew out demonstrations led by Martin Luther King, Jr., who emerged to national prominence with his epic "I Have a Dream" speech in August. King and his colleagues had learned a costly lesson in 1962 in Georgia in the Albany desegregation movement, widely regarded as a failure for civil rights, when they were outfoxed by local sheriff Laurie Pritchett. Like other sheriffs, Pritchett used mass arrests to break up demonstrations, but he dispersed protesters to several jails throughout southwest Georgia so that they wouldn't gain a sense of cohesion and momentum as the jails filled up. He also met nonviolent protest with nonviolent police action, scrupulously avoiding the negative publicity that would have derailed his genteel racist efficiency.

Birmingham was a different beast. The movement there had been spearheaded by local legend Rev. Fred Shuttlesworth, and King and his organization signed on to bring greater visibility to their efforts. Albany had taught King another lesson: not to go after segregation in general, but to target specific aspects for legal challenge. The Birmingham movement took aim at segregated facilities by boycotting large retail stores and lunch counters. As the activists mounted protests, more successfully than in Albany, they made an impact by getting arrested. But legal maneuvers by the state—especially ordering the city's bail bondsmen not to bail out jailed protesters and upping the maximum bail for a misdemeanor from $300 to $2,500— significantly dampened the movement. The adults faced reprisals at work, and their membership in civil rights groups was greatly frowned upon or outlawed. They were intimidated from participating in the protests, and the movement threatened to lull and diminish. It was then that the women, and then the youth, joined—first the college students, but when their numbers proved thin, a battalion of pre-teens and teenagers flooded the streets and jails in protest. Not even Bull Connor's pressure hoses and the snarling teeth of K-9s at their worst could dissuade them. When the evening news televised the horrors of hate across America's black-and-white screens, it jolted citizens and shocked the conscience of the nation. King and his colleagues hoped that their actions would not only deal a death blow to southern segregation but force Kennedy's hand to send a civil rights bill to Congress.

Birmingham was important for another reason: it was the first time "during the racial revolution of the 1960s that American Negroes assumed the role of the aggressors."[2] As a result, the "'rules of the game' in race relations were permanently changed." In the predawn hours of Mother's Day, 1963, in the telling phrase of historian Arthur Schlesinger, the "savage response" of angry blacks was glimpsed. Negroes hurled rocks, broke windows, burned down shops, and attacked police officers. They were reacting to the violent assault on black leadership after many of the movement leaders had suffered the bombing of their offices and homes: The home of A. D. King, the brother of Martin Luther King, had been bombed, as had the motel where King and other leaders were staying. Nevertheless, Birmingham changed the face and fate of the civil rights movement, hailing a new national leader in King and promising even greater victories on the streets and in the courts and Congress.

The president finally dispatched Burke Marshall to Birmingham to help start genuine conversations between the moderate business owners and the determined civil rights leadership. For their lukewarm efforts at racial justice (the brothers claimed interest in race but let the moment pass, and they spoke out of both sides of their political mouths to black leaders and conservative allies alike, doing little to move the racial needle), Jack and Bobby Kennedy became villains in the eyes of Dixiecrats—those southern Democrats who seceded from the party in 1948 in opposition to its support of civil rights—and white bigots who decried them as "nigger-lovers." In 1960, Jack Kennedy's perceived liberalness had made him vulnerable—he didn't win any electoral votes in Mississippi and only half the votes in Alabama. In 1963, the electoral math was even more fractured by the renewed perception that the Kennedys were too liberal. Democratic Party strategists began to craft a plan to win back disaffected white segregationists and the Kennedys were listening to them. As Robert Kennedy and the Negro elite met in May, the administration's once considerable cache among Negroes had been depleted by their spineless retreats.

The knowledge of the Kennedys' racial bipolarity wore heavy on many of the black participants in the Kennedy-Baldwin meeting. They understood the roughhouse politics that had to be played to maintain power. But they also understood that race was a defining issue, not just politically but morally, and that ultimately a president would have to take a stand for what was right, for what he truly believed in, and that he couldn't continue to survive by making a series of feints and hints toward true change while maintaining credibility among rabid racists.

It was common for white folk to tell their views to black folk: black people constantly, endlessly, helplessly listened, listened, listened, and then listened some more—as servants, friends, colleagues, and allies, even—to white folks' fears, desperation, and desires; their hopes, hates, and highs; their lows, too; their depression and exhilaration, their plans and pains, their utterly ordinary and unsurprisingly mediocre lives. They did so without pausing or being asked to speak of their own lives and fears, their own apprehensions and terrors, their own deferred dreams and chilling nightmares—the way something as simple as the slip of a tongue, the glance of an eye, a whistle might send them to their graves, disappearing into the very nothingness that white folk never noticed they had come from or would return to without fanfare or acclaim, without the gentle recognition of their humanity or magic or majestic ordinariness.

But on this day, in this meeting, something different happened: the unvarnished, unfiltered truth got loose; the reality of black perception without blinders or shades became clear; the beautiful ugliness of our existence got vented without being dressed up and made presentable, or amenable, or acceptable, to white ears. That's why that meeting made headlines, made the front page, made history, and, finally, made the white man listen.

* * *

Somehow Bobby Kennedy and Jimmy Baldwin seemed fated to end up in a room to hash out their contrasting, at times complementary, views of the world. Fate played a large role in Kennedy's life. He was the third of four boys in a family of nine children, and if birth order has any meaning, then Bobby's later arrival, and his slighter stature, weighed on him his entire life. As a runt, he was less confident than his older brothers Joseph Jr., a war hero who perished in World War II on a top-secret mission, and John, who inherited from his older brother their father's wish that he become president, which he did, but not before becoming a war hero too, and a congressman and senator. Bobby was forever in their shadows. The younger Kennedy fought hard to overcome a lonely childhood in which he felt invisible and inferior and, at times, isolated and excluded. The teeming despair of his early years would prove essential to Kennedy finally grasping, however tentatively, the way American apartheid punished black children and their families.[3]

What Bobby lacked in social stature and physical gifts, he compensated for in terms of a derring-do that teetered from raw courage to reckless endeavor. He took readily to an existentialist's creed of molding one's life out of the materials of the given time and space of one's days while clinging tenaciously to a Catholic faith in the Almighty, a faith put constantly in peril by the tragedies of the human plight. He was drawn to Greek philosophy and Shakespearean drama, which matched his gallows humor—witticism in the face of woe, poetry to placate the pain.

Even when Bobby was feeble-handed or anxious in the teeth of the overwhelming gravity of his duties, he trudged forward in the belief that although his path may have been predetermined, it would not continue without his input, without his Herculean effort to bend the curve of events in his favor, or, at least, the favor of those he served. Service was for him the price he willingly, lovingly paid for his position at home, where he catered to his imperious father, and, subsequently, in politics, where he served his commanding president brother Jack as attorney general. Bobby had remarkable courage and persistence, and he was not afraid to grow. Some of the change was dramatic: after being a loyal apologist for Joe McCarthy in the fifties he developed a tough-minded empathy for the genuinely less fortunate in the sixties. He eventually became a man that the masses could identify with. His appeal was wide: he was beloved by the dusty, impoverished stalwarts of Appalachia as well as by the desperately poor denizens of the inner city. An impressive swath of the ideological spectrum from left to right claimed him as inspiration and icon. But he also flashed signs of troubling racial sentiment. Even as a liberal there were corners of offense in his racist appeals to the white electorate. For instance, he trotted out a bit of racial paranoia when he declared in 1968 during the California primary that his Democratic rival Eugene McCarthy wanted to move 10,000 black folk into Orange County.[4]

If fate kept pace with Bobby, measured his gait, and dictated his political perambulation, then, to a degree, it fit the roots and rise of Jimmy Baldwin, too. Baldwin was born in Harlem, which is to say, in a mythological terrain that held great esteem among Negroes as the cultural epicenter of black America. Its streets were traversed by legendary figures like scholar W.E.B. Du Bois, actor Paul Robeson, singer Billie Holiday, anthropologist and writer Zora Neale Hurston, poet Langston Hughes, jazz composer and bandleader Duke Ellington, religious leader Father Divine, political activist Marcus Garvey, and a slew of other thinkers, entertainers, clergy, and cultural icons. There were colorful outlaws, too, like drug trafficker, bootlegger, and occasional pimp Bumpy Johnson, and Stephanie Saint-Clair, a mob boss at the helm of myriad criminal enterprises, most notably a numbers empire. Baldwin was born, and reborn, for a spell at least, in the Holiness-Pentecostal church, and cut his teeth as a boy preacher at the Fireside Pentecostal Assembly storefront church. The cult of moralism, and the culture of respectability, mixed with white supremacists' blistering attacks on black culture as the source of evil and ethical perversion. Baldwin internalized the withering self-scrutiny and moral debasement of the extreme forms of belief embraced by many black Pentecostal adherents.

Baldwin's preaching had a lasting impact. The language of the King James Bible sounds throughout his verbal universe. Baldwin's stately eloquence and formal precision defeat the belief that black folk are dull and inarticulate. He drank deeply from Western literacy and it washed over his vast learning. Henry James left his mark on Baldwin's prose in the rhythm of his sentences and the impressionistic portraits of experience. But the emotional and moral center of black existence flamed in his rhetoric too. Fire burned in his literary craft: cleansing, purifying fire, the kind that burst into tongues in his Pentecostal youth, and the hot moral fire of his social prophecy. Jimmy raged against the dying of the moral light and fought fire with fire by unleashing his fury on the racial hell from which he sought to deliver our nation.

Baldwin, like Bobby, was diminutive and, more than that, experienced the vulnerability, and vitality, of being gay. Besides the hostility it evoked, his queerness draped his frame, inflected his speech, and added zest to his verbal flourishes. He was a black man who believed at first that he was ugly, just as he had been told in his youth, but discovered, belatedly, that he wasn't ugly after all. His ugliness disappeared when our disdain for Negro noses and lips got shown for what it is: a hatred of the black self that often scars the black psyche.

And like Bobby, Baldwin had forsaken the God of his youth, only to discover a richer register of love that echoed through his sentences and fed the heart of his witness and prophecy. Baldwin, the grandson of an enslaved man—and surely that fact haunted him and opened up worlds of possibility, too, since it gave him purchase on a history that seemed ancient to others— was obsessed with love because it had eluded him: at times at home, with a brutal, self-hating stepfather; at times among jealous black writers and intellectuals; and even among civil rights leaders he admired, like Martin Luther King, Jr.

King complained in a conversation secretly captured by the FBI of appearing with Jimmy on television; he was "put off by the poetic exaggeration in Baldwin's approach to race issues."[5] But, like Bobby, Baldwin persisted. He ran off to France, and eventually Turkey, seeking less polluted racial air, but returned to fight shoulder-to-shoulder with his comrades at home. And all the while he was writing, speaking, thinking, loving, refusing to give in to despair, but driven, often, by a hopeful hopelessness that secured his appeal among whites who depended on his criticism of the present as an affirmation of a possible future, and among the vast congregation of black folk who loved God and couldn't understand why evil often prevailed but were afraid to ask. Baldwin, the lapsed Pentecostal, was their preacher, speaking elegantly of the chaotic truths that ganged up on precious souls trying to make heads or tails of existence, in the same way that Bobby, a chastened Catholic, was the mouthpiece for millions who struggled with faith in service of truth.

It was only a matter of time before these warriors for justice converged, and it was perhaps even inevitable that they collided. The sparks that flew from their meeting lit a fire in Bobby that quietly burned until his death five years later, a fire that also warmed Baldwin again to truths closer to home.

* * *

If John Kennedy was at best ambivalent about civil rights at the start of his presidency, he was increasingly drawn into the fray as racial catastrophes tested his will to use federal authority or the bully pulpit to protect civil rights for black citizens. His choices for the federal bench in the South often defied decency and the just application of law to black people. He appointed federal judges like Mississippi's Harold Cox—who from the bench rejected the Justice Department's bid to register Negroes to vote by calling aspiring black voters "a bunch of niggers"—and refused to combat segregated schooling. Beyond political and legal quandaries, there was the moral dimension of race to consider, too: black people were more committed each year to aggressively challenging the vicious and dishonorable faces of southern apartheid and northern racism. President Kennedy consulted his cabinet and advisers to determine what minimal efforts he could make toward racial progress without undermining his political survival.

As attorney general, Robert Kennedy took many cues from his brother, but he also sought to chart his own path. Early 1963 had been tough going for Bobby, who orbited his brother John Kennedy's presidential universe with increasing confidence in his mission to bring racial justice to America. He believed that black suffrage would be achieved, black employment would be boosted, and that black and white folk could eat at the same restaurants, attend the same concerts, and ride public transportation seated next to each other. He also believed that the races would one day go to school together. To be sure, Bobby, like his older brother, only slowly came to understand how best to aid a country afflicted by one racial crisis after the next—from forcing universities to accept Negro students to trying to stem the tide of grief and violence brewing in ghettoes because of police brutality.

Kennedy sought to tamp down racial skirmishes that threatened to combust into civil war, encouraging comity amidst desperate violence, holding up the virtue of moderation over militancy. He agreed that voting would become a central means to freedom for black folk. He momentarily got J. Edgar Hoover to loosen his hold on hoary bigotry and hire more black folk at the FBI. And he attended to the birth of new black freedom in the South in 1963 like a legal midwife as he sought to protect Freedom Riders in Alabama and James Meredith's lonely moral crusade to lay stakes in hallowed Confederate ground by integrating Mississippi's flagship university. He also worked behind the scenes with Martin Luther King, Jr., in Birmingham to forge a settlement of grievances, getting local white leaders to agree to a moderate level of desegregation and black employment and a lessening of hostilities in that fervid epicenter of racial violence.

Yet Bobby was a creature of his time. There were tremendous forces at war inside him, forces that not only tore at his soul but threatened to tear the nation asunder. Bobby both embodied and undercut the status quo: he was an everyman that progressive white folk could identify with, and he was a white leader whose genuinely good intentions were at odds with his naked political ambition.

But Jimmy Baldwin had had enough. He had been crisscrossing the country on barnstorming lecture

tours trying to tell America about the scourge of racism and the hateful social practices, like Jim Crow,
that grew from the myths of whiteness. Baldwin had
seen on television, with the rest of the world, the car-
toonish barbarism of Birmingham public safety com-
missioner Bull Connor as he directed goons with
badges and guns to thrash black flesh. Connor aimed
high-pressure hoses at protesters, including children,
hoping to wash them from the American conscience
while snarling police dogs bit at their flesh.

On May 12, 1963, Baldwin dashed off a blistering
cable to Attorney General Robert F. Kennedy.

> THOSE WHO BEAR THE GREATEST RESPONSIBILITY FOR
> THE CHAOS IN BIRMINGHAM ARE NOT IN BIRMINGHAM.
> AMONG THOSE RESPONSIBLE ARE J. EDGAR HOOVER,
> SENATOR EASTLAND [of Mississippi], THE POWER
> STRUCTURE WHICH HAS GIVEN BULL CONNOR SUCH LI-
> CENSE, AND PRESIDENT KENNEDY, WHO HAS NOT USED
> THE GREAT PRESTIGE OF HIS OFFICE AS THE MORAL FO-
> RUM WHICH IT CAN BE. THIS CRISIS IS NEITHER REGIONAL
> NOR RACIAL. IT IS A MATTER OF THE NATION'S LIFE OR
> DEATH. NO TRUCE CAN BE BINDING UNTIL THE AMERI-
> CAN PEOPLE AND OUR REPRESENTATIVES ARE ABLE TO
> ACCEPT THE SIMPLE FACT THAT THE NEGRO IS A MAN.[6]

The white betrayal in Birmingham proved little
match for the dramatic fury of Martin Luther King, Jr.,

who put children and women in harm's way to high-light the depravity of Connor, and by extension, a society that made him possible. It wasn't just Connor who had to go; it was the way of life that supported such a figure and others, like rabid segregationist Governor George Wallace, who stood in the doorway of the University of Alabama not only to block the entry of students, but in truth to block the future. In fact, King was deeply disappointed in the foot-dragging approach of the Kennedy administration to civil rights legislation.

However, Bobby was energized after he and Burke Marshall drew big praise from King and Andrew Young for helping to broker the Birmingham resolution. Flush with victory, Kennedy understandably felt confident in his ability to dig deeper into the race problem behind the scenes.

Baldwin's telegrammed missive came at just the right time. Kennedy was wary at that moment of black leadership—he couldn't so easily persuade King and some of the younger activists to rethink the volume and timing of their direct action—and Baldwin seemed just the sort of independent voice who might help explain what was going on in black America.

Baldwin was then the biggest, hottest black figure in the nation, indeed, the most celebrated writer of any color in the land. He had become, overnight, *the* spokesman for Negroes, and eventually he would put his literary career on hold for a time in order to

herald the racial Armageddon that awaited the nation
should it not heed his voice and pay attention to militant students and prophets like Martin Luther King,
Jr. He had just appeared on the cover of *Time* magazine, and Bobby had read his moving, searing missive in *The New Yorker* that became the bulk of *The
Fire Next Time,* a poignant bestseller and instant classic that depicted the harrowing conditions that most
black folk in the nation faced. Baldwin gave voice to
the experiences of millions of Negroes in America in
a way that didn't retreat from the rage that besieged
black communities.

Bobby had already been meeting with various
groups and figures to sound out the prospects for racial change.[7] In one of these confidential briefings, the
comedian Dick Gregory had suggested that Kennedy
connect with the brilliant young writer. Kennedy and
Baldwin weren't total strangers. They had met briefly
at the White House the year before at a dinner for No-
bel Prize laureates and agreed that they would like to
talk more. In light of this, and Baldwin's telegram, the
attorney general was eager to meet with the writer.
Baldwin received a message through his agent, Bob
Mills, to call Kennedy aide Burke Marshall, who issued an invitation to breakfast with Kennedy the following morning at his Hickory Hill estate in McLean,
Virginia. Baldwin accepted. He capped off the day
with typically furious activity: a dinner in his honor

followed by a lecture at Wesleyan University, then an hour-long conversation with members of a fraternity, then a series of nightcaps at his sponsor's apartment, and barely two hours of sleep. The next morning, he and his agent caught the 7:00 a.m. shuttle to Washington. Baldwin's plane was late, but they were nevertheless greeted by Kennedy's Negro chauffeur. Baldwin shook his hand, and off they went.

They shared a breakfast of poached eggs and coffee. Kennedy quizzed Baldwin about the Black Muslims, and Baldwin responded that the Negro's situation in the North was so dire that their despair left them vulnerable to the extremist organization's appeal.

"Who are the Negroes other Negroes listen to, do you think?" Kennedy asked. "Not politicians. I don't mean Adam Clayton Powell. Or even Martin Luther King."

Baldwin insisted that Negroes would listen to folk like playwright Lorraine Hansberry, entertainers Lena Horne and Harry Belafonte, social psychologist Kenneth Clark, and the Freedom Riders.

"Look, I'd like to meet them."

Baldwin agreed to try to gather them on Kennedy's behalf.

The Kennedy children hadn't yet eaten breakfast and they interrupted the conversation a couple of times to speak to their father. Baldwin hadn't touched his bacon so Kennedy promptly parceled out the pieces to his hungry children. Baldwin silently observed the interaction with affection. Perhaps he hoped that in the coming generation many more white folk could do as Kennedy did: sit as an equal at the breakfast table with a black man. That would signal real racial change.

After one of the interruptions, Baldwin placed his cup on the table and proclaimed that black folk wanted to be treated like citizens, like Americans, that they wanted their president to be far more aggressive on civil rights, seeing it not primarily as a political matter but as a moral issue. Kennedy insisted that the president had done just that in his message to Congress in January, when the New York newspapers had been out on strike, and that he'd get Baldwin a copy of President Kennedy's remarks.

Breakfast lasted only half an hour, having started late. Bobby had to rush off to another appointment, but not before he surprised his maid and introduced her to Baldwin. She was thrilled.

"You'll probably want his autograph, won't you?" Kennedy asked.

"Oh, yes!" she exclaimed.

"Why don't you get the copy of *Time* that has Mr. Baldwin's picture on the cover?" Kennedy thoughtfully suggested. "There's one upstairs in the bedroom."

She hurried upstairs and retrieved the magazine and Baldwin graciously scribbled his signature over Boris Chaliapin's cover portrait of him.

Like the words of Martin Luther King, Baldwin's words had already wormed their way into Bobby's vexed racial thinking. He tried to diminish their power by acting as if it were black folks who were most directly impacted by Baldwin's writing. Hence the suggestion that the maid would want Baldwin's autograph on the magazine that sat by *Kennedy*'s bed.

As they hastily drove into the city, Kennedy chatted with Baldwin a bit more and asked if they could meet the following afternoon in his father's Manhattan apartment. Mills whipped out his pad to take down the address.

"I don't know it," Kennedy admitted. "One advantage of being an Attorney General is that you don't need to remember your address—you can call someone on the phone and ask." Marshall gave them the address. Both Kennedy and Baldwin recalled liking each other in later interviews.[8]

"We had a very nice meeting," Kennedy said.

"I was really quite impressed by him," Baldwin remarked.

Baldwin agreed to organize an impromptu gathering.

"So I said okay, not quite realizing what I'd gotten myself into," Baldwin remembered. "I called up a few friends."

As important as the meeting was, one might reasonably conclude that Baldwin gave profound consideration to the guest list. While he had a few folk in mind, it was the luck of the draw: who of Baldwin's high-profile friends or acquaintances happened to be available the next afternoon. Fortunately, some of the folk he had mentioned on the spot to Kennedy agreed to assemble.

* * *

Beyond what chance brought them, Baldwin and Kennedy were on the same page when it came to getting black folk in that room who hadn't been deputized by a civil rights group and therefore were not beholden to official and safe lines of thought. In broad strokes, beyond the folk with ordinary jobs—including Baldwin's secretary, Edward False, his brother David, and David's friend Thais Aubrey; and white people like his agent, Mills, and the television producer Henry Morgenthau III, proving his democratic instincts as much as his desire to fill the room—Baldwin also called on his attorney, Clarence Jones, who doubled as Martin Luther King's lawyer; the white actor Rip Torn; and the Chicago Urban League head, Edwin Berry, all of whom reflected his threefold calling as an artist, intellectual, and activist.

But the boldface names shone the brightest. Harry Belafonte was a magical artist who commanded the music charts and attracted women by the droves as a matinee idol. As a black star with a light complexion,

Belafonte had projected onto his golden dewy skin the sexually charged desire to escape the cage that consigned darker-skinned blacks to the bin of the less desirable, the less beautiful, the less glorious. But Belafonte seemed at once to revel in the privilege that came his way and to undercut it with his radical politics. Like many yellow leaders and notable men who boasted of roots in the Caribbean, from Malcolm X to Louis Farrakhan, Belafonte turned his socially bestowed racial privilege into a bully pulpit on behalf of the black masses. Belafonte also delighted in the signifying and code-switching that were common to blacks who lived among the white masses, where black survival depended on the skill to mask one's true cultural beliefs and political intents. When Belafonte undulated to Calypso, when he belted a show tune or a folk song, he was delivering an emancipatory message through the medium that allowed him to be smooth and seductive, and yet, at the same time, slick and political. If the liberating example of Paul Robeson compelled Belafonte to sing a song so that the masses could be inspired, Robeson's suffering warned Belafonte to proceed with care around the powers that be. Belafonte learned, like so many black artists learned, to hide in plain sight. And yet he exulted in racial uplift; he took great pleasure in using all of his resources to bring black folk that much closer to the promised land looming so far in the distant future. And he was a dependable superstar, a black man who took pains to be at the ready to lead a march, sing a song at a fundraiser, donate thousands to a worthy cause, and pour his considerable wealth and time into the effort to support black leadership as it sought to emancipate black people.

Belafonte had been wary of coming because he didn't want anything the group said to undermine King and other civil rights leaders. He was joined that day by Lena Horne, another remarkable personality, who had a different reason to be leery. Horne was one of the biggest stars in black America, and one of its most beautiful women. She starred on the silver screen and made recordings with her velvety vocals. Like Belafonte, her lighter skin got her artistic purchase where darker-skinned black women were relegated to playing mammies or sardonic Sapphires. But Horne had been less inclined to meld social conscience and popular expression. She was always gracious and generous, but she had been far less secure about how her skill and skin might be read inside black political circles and far less likely early on to make the sort of sacrifices that Belafonte had made. But as she matured, and gained a sense of her artistic independence and racial self-confidence, Horne was much more receptive to the idea of being a social activist while maintaining her perch in Hollywood and in the recording booth. Her stunning good looks became a kind of political force in their own way: her blinding smile and her sublime beauty softened the blows she struck as she became more outspoken.

Horne undoubtedly benefited from the insight and wisdom of another woman who attended the meeting that day, the playwright Lorraine Hansberry. Feted for her artistic gifts, she was adept at fusing the ferocious political will she had imbibed in her girlhood home from her father with the growing sense she had that gender was just as important as race in determining how black women made it in the world. (Hansberry was, in her time, one of the most celebrated black playwrights in history, the first black to win a New York Drama Critics Circle Award.) She translated her ideological affinities into palatable language to articulate progressive ideas about family and money. Although she spent most of her brief life in the closet as a queer woman, Hansberry turned on her powerful introspection to light a path for other women and men who felt out of sorts, lost, without a rudder or anchor. If Belafonte had learned to disguise his most radical political sensibilities, so had Hansberry, perhaps even more so, as she literally used the mundane domestic scene of black American life in her monumental play *A Raisin in the Sun* to subtly deliver some powerful insight about how capital and its lack—well, really, its inaccessible abundance—ruin the social ambitions of the vulnerable black working class.

Hansberry had been an activist long before Baldwin and had taught him more than a little about how to effectively express political passion while maintaining artistic integrity. She protested for the integration of local institutions, headed a leftist political organization, and even campaigned for the progressive presidential candidate Henry Wallace. Hansberry later joined the Communist Party and helped Paul Robeson produce a black radical journal titled *Freedom*. After she married fellow artist Robert Nemiroff, and then divorced him, she began to grapple with the unwieldy convergences of gender, race, sexuality, and class in a life that is surely one of the first and finest examples of modern intersectionality in the land.[9]

But she wasn't the meeting's only pioneer. Before there was any talk of black public intellectuals, Kenneth Clark fulfilled the function. He was a first-rate scholar who brought an old-world prestige to the academy and to the field outside the lecture hall. Clark was one of the first scholar-activists to meld his ambition to do world-class social science with a desire to change the world he studied. After earning a doctorate in psychology from Columbia University, he became a prominent figure in the post–World War II civil rights movement. He fought white supremacy with his pen, but he also waged combat against cultural ignorance by advising congressional committees, speaking tirelessly across the country, and writing influential books and articles. Clark wrote about the ghetto and thus pioneered the sociological investigation of urban poverty and class deprivation from a social psychological perspective. Clark and his wife, Mamie, also a gifted scholar, devised their doll test—showing how even black kids preferred white rather than black dolls—to prove that the psychology of race penetrated fragile black minds and lured them into their own self-denigration. But his research, analysis, and expert testimony for the *Brown v. Board of Education* case was much deeper and far more expansive and embraced a wide-ranging empirical examination of the psychological and social factors that reinforced prejudice and the politics of bigotry.

These four artists, activists, and intellectuals made the meeting a touchstone of black genius in the service of black struggle for freedom, equality, and self-determination. Yet they all had the humility to recognize that Jerome Smith, a Freedom Rider, was the most important witness to black struggle in their midst. He happened to be in town receiving medical treatment for his vicious beatings at the hands of white hooligans, those in uniform and out.

Baldwin met his brother David, a one-time singer; Jerome Smith; and Lorraine Hansberry in his agent's office before heading over to the Kennedy family's tony digs at 24 Central Park South. It was the same lavish apartment where Martin Luther King, Jr., had his first face-to-face meeting with presidential candidate John F. Kennedy in 1960.

When Baldwin's coterie arrived they found Lena Horne and Rip Torn waiting in the lobby. Horne had flown in from California and got there first. When the doorman announced that no one was home, she settled on a ledge, and, when Torn arrived, chatted with him until the others showed up. Bobby finally appeared with Burke Marshall and his press aide Ed Guthman, and they all headed upstairs. The group helped themselves to light refreshments. Then Bobby took the floor.

Kennedy was hamstrung from the start.[10] First, there was the motley crew of folk amassed before him. It was a risk; many curious and conscientious celebrities were not used to deep political analysis and the rigors of drilling down to the unsexy bottom of public policy. Second, he was party to the geography of race that sliced a segregated line through the room with whites on one side, Negroes on the other. "The character of the meeting was symbolized by the seating arrangements," Lena Horne said. It was a small, symbolic act, to be sure, but in the realm of race, such gestures gather cumulative force and either stimulate or stymie change. The separation of races had become all too familiar, unquestioned, and thus natural; so natural that even among well-heeled Negro and white elites, the corrosive social order they were all pledged to defeat crept into that room.

Kennedy began informally, taking off his jacket and rolling up his sleeves. He sat in a straight-back chair and shared a bit of banter with Belafonte, a frequent guest at Hickory Hill. Belafonte asked about Ethel Kennedy, Bobby's pregnant wife. Kennedy joked that the baby might get Belafonte booted out of his room. Some of Belafonte's peers that afternoon thought that the star might have been quietly reprimanding himself for having failed to already tell Bobby Kennedy of the anger and heartbreak that gripped black America. But Belafonte remembers feeling mostly suspicious.

"I was concerned that high-profile people would say things that Bobby Kennedy might eventually use against Dr. King," Belafonte told me.

Kennedy started by listing all the important and pioneering things the Kennedy administration had done on behalf of Negroes and civil rights. In truth, it wasn't hard to do more than any previous administration, because the effort and energy devoted to civil rights had up to that point been simply abysmal. And, as noted, despite Bobby's bragging, the Kennedy administration had a well-deserved reputation among civil rights devotees for doing as little as possible to enflame southern white bigots as they tiptoed around the prospect of equal rights for Negroes. Many black folk understood the need to be circumspect, but the Kennedy administration chronically frustrated the quest for justice. Still, as Lena Horne said, most Negroes there were willing to offer the Kennedys a presumption of honest effort and good will. Calling Kennedy's reactions that day "defensive," Horne wrote in her autobiography that despite the attempt of the administration to help, so much more was needed.

> The funny thing was that no one there disputed [the administration's efforts]. It was just that it did not seem enough, especially in light of all the history that had gone before. We all wanted more. Many of us told him that we were grateful for the strong stand the government had just taken on getting James Meredith into the University of Mississippi. It was accepted as evidence of good faith—otherwise none of us would have been there—but he didn't realize how much we expected of him and how much more we felt had to be done, and quickly.

In a message that could be ripped from today's headlines, Kennedy warned the gathering that race would play a big role in the next election in 18 months. "We have a party in revolt," Kennedy said, "and we have to be somewhat considerate about how to keep

them onboard if the Democratic Party is going to prevail in the next elections." Hence the dilemma black
voters perpetually face: how to effectively argue for
their just reward for loyalty to a party that often takes
them for granted while keeping its eye on the disaffected white voter who might potentially bail in resentment of the few benefits offered to black folk. Like
so many white Americans, Kennedy wanted the Negroes to be grateful for slow and steady improvement.
But Negroes were done with gratitude and gradualism. King had lashed out earlier that year at the idea
of going in a moderate direction at a measured pace in
his famous "Letter from a Birmingham Jail." Later that
year, in his epic "I Have a Dream" address in Washington, D.C., he would warn that this was "no time to
engage in the luxury of cooling off or to take the tran-
quilizing drug of gradualism." He trumpeted, instead,
"the fierce urgency of now." Negroes embraced aspiration and achievement.

Kennedy argued that instead of acknowledging the
looming political crisis and saluting the administration's actions, black folk were being seduced by extremist elements in black America and listening to the siren
song of the Black Muslims. And that spelled trouble.

"You don't have no idea what trouble is," Jerome
Smith interjected. His exclamation sent a chill through
the room.

But he was just getting started.

"Because I'm close to the moment where I'm ready to take up a gun. I've seen what government can do to crush the spirit and lives of people in the South."

Lorraine Hansberry spoke up for Smith, dismaying Kennedy.

"Lorraine Hansberry said that [she and her comrades] were going to go down and get guns," Bobby later recalled, "and they were going to give the guns to people on the street, and they were going to start to kill white people."[11]

Perhaps Hansberry was taking poetic license in dramatically overstating the case. Smith's sentiments, however, were decidedly nonfiction and thus even more terrifying to Bobby.

Smith's statement was genuinely astonishing. He was a follower of Gandhi and King, a devotee of nonviolent protest in the service of black freedom. He was no doctrinaire black radical given to the exercise of his Second Amendment right to bear arms, but he could no longer bear the pain of calculated indifference to the trauma that black people endured every day.

Kennedy surely had not anticipated such an outburst, and neither had the other participants. And yet Smith had the immediate respect and admiration of his black peers, who realized that they lacked his compelling authenticity, his existential credence. Smith had endured the most exacting revenge by law enforcement for the desire to be free. He had few rivals other than John Lewis in enduring so many beatings, bearing in his body the aftereffects of grievous violence toward blackness.

"I don't know what I'm doing here, listening to all this cocktail-party patter," Smith said, shattering the comity of the room—a comity, however, built on dishonesty, which is no comity at all. Smith was having none of it. He insisted it wasn't the Black Muslims who were the problem. Their apolitical bearing meant they ultimately weren't much of a threat; they risked little, and therefore they put no pressure on the status quo. Black folk knew who was willing to die for the cause. Malcolm X may have spurned Martin Luther King for putting women and children in harm's way in Birmingham, but Smith knew that Malcolm's words rang hollow because neither he nor his followers were willing to take their place. Because Smith was a devotee of nonviolence who was quickly losing his faith, he was a far graver threat to the social order than the Black Muslims who had never made such a pledge.

"When *I* pull the trigger, kiss it goodbye."

After his earlier emotional tempest, Bobby bitterly accepted his fate that day and silently seethed. He would find no rescue from grief through an understanding black pat on the back, no soothing black voice to qualify the anger, at least not until the meeting was done and Belafonte and Jones attempted to offer him consolation.

Kennedy had never witnessed black pain like this before, in such naked, unglossed ferocity. That meant that he had never really seen *them,* his fellow black citizens, not honestly. The black folk in the room had largely let the rage run free, for a moment at least, before one of the most powerful white men in the world. The moment justified Baldwin's observation that to "be a Negro in this country and to be relatively conscious is to be in a rage almost all the time."[12]

Smith's effect was amplified, ironically, because he possessed a speech impediment which intensified when he was agitated. He let it be known that just the thought of having to be in that room, pleading for his rights, pleading for what white folk could take for granted at birth, made him want to throw up.

"I knew what he meant," said Baldwin. "It was not personal at all. If you'd been in Birmingham, and on those highways and in those jails waiting for the Justice Department or the FBI to act, you'd be nauseated too."[13]

Feeling under siege, Kennedy tried to ignore Smith and turn to more reasonable voices and cooler heads. But it was too late. The participants weren't falling prey to the white liberal ruse of seeking moderating influences to prevail over seemingly hotheaded catharsis. Baldwin says it was a mistake for Kennedy to pivot "toward us . . . the reasonable, responsible, mature representatives of the black community."[14]

Hansberry spoke up: "You've got a great many very accomplished people in this room, Mr. Attorney General. But the only man you should be listening to is that man over there." With that decisive rejection of respectability politics, she sealed Kennedy's fate. He would be forced to finally hear instead of speak, to listen instead of lecture. But he wasn't ready to surrender yet.

When Baldwin, perhaps deliberately ratcheting up the discord, asked Smith if he were willing to go to Cuba to fight—the CIA's failed military invasion of Cuba, termed the Bay of Pigs, had taken place in April 1961—and defend American interests, Smith hurled his answer with striking bitterness: "Never! Never! Never!"

His volcanic eruption brought Bobby to the edge.

"You will not fight for your country?" Bobby asked Smith in disbelief. "How can you say that?" One of Bobby's brothers died in war; a second brother, now the president, had nearly perished too. This tapped a deeply personal vein with Bobby. And yet not even this could dissuade Smith from hammering Kennedy's beloved if naïve patriotism.

"What you're asking us young black people to do is pick up guns against people [in other countries] while you have continued to deny us our rights here."

The urban agenda Kennedy had hoped to address in the meeting suffered a gut punch of black rage. The seismic shift in mood in black America registered that day, not only in Smith's catalytic anger, but in the agreement of all the black folk there that Smith, and not the artists or intellectuals, should be listened to. Lena Horne captured it in searing prose in her autobiography.

> You could not encompass his anger, his fury, in a set of statistics, nor could Mr. Belafonte and Dr. Clark and Miss Horne, the fortunate Negroes, who had never been in a Southern jail, keep up the pretense of being the mature, responsible spokesmen for the race any more. All of a sudden the fancy phrases like "depressed area" and "power structure" and all the rest were nothing. It seemed to me that day that this boy just put it like it was. He communicated the plain, basic suffering of being a Negro. The primeval memory of everyone in that room went to work after that. We all went back to nitty-gritty with that kid who was out there in a cotton patch trying to get poor, miserable Negro people not to be scared to sign their names to a piece of paper saying they'd vote. We were back at the level where a man just wants to be a man, living and breathing, where unless he has that right, all the rest is only talk.

Baldwin agreed. Smith "became the focal point. I think that threw Kennedy. That boy, after all, in some sense, represented everybody in that room . . . Our honor. Our dignity. But, above all, our hope."[15]

Kennedy fumed more as the rest of the room closed in on him and piled on argument after argument. When Baldwin suggested that President Kennedy make a dramatic gesture by escorting a black student to a desegregated school, or by accompanying the two black students whom Governor George Wallace had threatened to bar, Kennedy protested.

"No. This would be senseless. This would be phony."

When the black folk denounced the FBI, Kennedy and Marshall insisted that Department of Justice lawyers were taking up the slack of negligent agents.

"This answer produced almost hysterical laughter," Clark remembers.

When Kennedy declared that he had worked closely with King behind the scenes, the jeers and shrieks could barely be muffled.

"That's not true."

Very shortly the verbal jousting and mutual recrimination silenced Kennedy. Bobby seemed worn down by the feisty resistance of his insurgent interlocutors; he appeared dazed, and not a little resentful, by the realization that he was on the wrong side of the debate, perhaps the wrong side of history. For the balance of the nearly three hours he just listened.

"It really was one of the most violent, emotional verbal assaults and attacks that I had ever witnessed," Clark recalled. "Bobby sat immobile in the chair. He no longer continued to defend himself. He just sat, and you could see the tension and the pressure building in him."

One can imagine what was said. This was a time of enormous frustration at the slow pace of racial change. The North was every bit as besieged by racial tensions as the South. Black rage was festering in northern streets where black folk were being denied educational and employment opportunities under an ostensibly non-racist government and society. Baldwin and his compatriots no doubt hammered Kennedy about the noblesse oblige of supposedly enlightened northern liberals who hadn't a clue about the extent of black suffering right beneath their noses. The group of black activists and artists no doubt scolded Kennedy for thinking he could play the honorary black man card, too—thinking that he could pull off the "white negro" shtick that Baldwin had already deconstructed in his friend and bitter rival Norman Mailer. They surely pelted the attorney general for failing to grapple with the despair that threatened to drown black America, a despair that was, even if inadvertently, perpetuated by the Kennedy administration's refusal to face race head-on.

There had to be great anger at just how manipulative and duplicitous the Kennedys had been in playing both sides of the racial divide against each other. Baldwin made a career of unmasking white privilege, too, and this surely rubbed Bobby raw, especially since he lacked the vocabulary to acknowledge his own white privilege, despite being Irish, and therefore a minority of sorts within the borders of whiteness. And the group surely shot Bobby down when it appeared that he was attempting to listen to black folk without trying to figure out how he could apply what he learned to make concrete institutional changes. His approach to the meeting that day was utilitarian rather than introspective, and even though Bobby was more likely than Jack to be open to such an encounter, he lacked the tools to pull it off successfully.

In fact, the brutal battering he suffered at the hands of the Baldwin crew offers an important lesson to white people about how to start real change. And that involves sometimes sitting silently, and, finally, as black folk have been forced to do, listening, and listening, and listening, and listening some more.

When the meeting was over, when most of the folk had filed out, Harry Belafonte and Clarence Jones, each in turn, privately expressed appreciation for the efforts of Kennedy and his brother to right things for the American Negro. Kennedy was miffed and tersely communicated his disappointment that neither had spoken up for him to the group when it mattered most. Belafonte and Jones suggested that had they come to Kennedy's defense they would have compromised their standing with the group and lessened their ability to move them along a path closer to their mutual agenda. At that moment Kennedy thought the meeting had been a huge waste of time. He wasn't the only one to think that. Most of the participants felt the meeting was a colossal failure.

"They don't know what the laws are," Kennedy raged. "They don't know what the facts are—they don't know what we've been doing or what we're trying to do. You can't talk to them the way you can talk to Martin Luther King or Roy Wilkins. They didn't want to talk that way.

"It was all emotion, hysteria—they stood up and orated—they cursed—some of them wept and left the room."

Kennedy drew the conclusion that he was interested in policy, and the blacks, with the exception of Clark and Berry, were interested in witness. The truth is they were done with half-hearted policies that failed to grapple with the terror of black existence; they were tired of the nuts and bolts of public policy that lacked a sense of the world such policies had to work in, a world where the hatred of blackness could never be solved solely by a governmental program.

The meeting highlighted the rage that had taken hold in large quarters of black America—a rage ignited by the persistent mistreatment of black folk, which continues, tragically, to this day. As does the fight over public policy and prophetic witness. Our politicians have often left us in the lurch, showing little support for substantive social change.

Bobby was angry that day, but in short order, the encounter with this group of extraordinary black folk would begin to haunt him; it would help change his mind and therefore history. But at first Bobby was petulant, self-pitying, and vengeful. Seething at his inglorious drubbing by the group, Bobby lashed out after the meeting, in private, to an aide. Bobby hurled an epithet at Baldwin for his homosexuality, and charged that Clarence Jones had acted out of guilt because he was married to a white woman.[16] On the record, Kennedy argued that a "number of them . . . I think, have complexes about the fact that they've been successful," that "they've done so well and this poor boy had been beaten by the police." Kennedy believed that survivor guilt made them think "that they really hadn't done their best . . . hadn't done what they should have done for the Negro." Thus, they had to upbraid him as a show of solidarity. "So the way to show that they

hadn't forgotten where they came from was to berate me and berate the United States government."[17]
After their meeting, Bobby called Baldwin a "nut."
The FBI also collected 1,884 pages on him, much of
it after Kennedy's anger at their encounter led him to
start, or continue, the FBI's snooping on many of the
attendees that day. Eventually Bobby got over his hurt
feelings and began to reflect more honestly on what
had happened.

"The meeting with James Baldwin was crucial,"
said reformed racist turned Freedom Rider and religion professor John Maguire.[18] "After Baldwin, he
was absolutely shocked," declared Nicholas Katzen-
bach, a former deputy attorney general who succeeded
Bobby when he became a New York senator. "Bobby
expected to be made an honorary black. [The meet-
ing] really hurt his feelings, and it was pretty mean.
But the fact that he thought he knew so much—and
learned he didn't—was important."[19] Bobby turned
his resentment to resolve and got even more determined to make substantive change, restructuring the
Justice Department's hiring practices to be more racially just and pushing his brother John to craft more
compelling civil rights legislation and to speak more
forthrightly about race.[20] Bobby developed what critic
Steve Levingston terms "understanding through empathy," making the leap, as Kennedy biographer Evan
Thomas argues, "from contempt to identification."[21]

Bobby confessed to his press secretary Edward Guthman that he might react like Jerome Smith if he had
endured similar trauma: "I guess if I were in his shoes,
if I had gone through what he's gone through, I might
feel differently about this country."[22]

Whatever his faults, or limits, Bobby Kennedy
was committed to getting into a room and wrestling
with the demons of race. Over 50 years later, we find it
hard to follow his example, and our failure dooms us
to untold suffering.

THE POLITICIANS

WHITENESS AND THE STATE

When Robert Kennedy met with James Baldwin and his friends, he weathered a heady downpour of racial and political truths that we still confront today: that politics, and the state, exist to defend white interests and identities; that witness is an important means to express black grievance and resistance and to shape public policy; that dormant and resurgent white bigotry, even at the highest level of government, must be identified and opposed; and that a new politics must be formed to fulfill true democracy.

The figures in that room made it there because they had made it in America. They had done so despite being denied everything Bobby could take for granted: justice, the benefit of the social and moral doubt, and ample incentives to believe the nation is great. The republic that Kennedy was willing to die for had had a hand in killing the ancestors and friends of his black compatriots. The men who fashioned democracy portrayed African people in America as threats to the cause of building a nation. They questioned African Americans' humanity and their intelligence, so that even after they got freedom, black people would be found without merit in the claim to citizenship.[1]

Both formal political culture and informal cultural politics reflected the will of the nation to negate the existence of black folk. Enslaving black people allowed whites to exploit their labor while denying their bodies legitimate rights. Black bodies had no "inalienable rights"; they existed at the pleasure and permission of white society. Laws and covenants, compacts and contracts, folkways and mores, institutions and civic culture existed for the benefit of white folk—to concretely realize their moral and social aspirations and to serve as ready reference of their norms and ideals. There was robust argument among white folk about how and when these norms and ideals should apply. But they agreed that the circumference of their newly forged civilization should exclude blacks, natives, and a rolling cast of "others." Nativist thinking and xenophobic instincts were baked into the framework of society. These notions were also central to a Constitution that declared each of the enslaved to be counted as three-fifths of a white inhabitant of a state. These ideas also cropped up in the Declaration of Independence, which saw Africans as "domestic in-surrectionists" and Indians as "merciless savages."

To be sure, black folk found room to breathe within the smothering confines of white society. They crafted an existence outside of the slavish demand for total surrender. But their lives were controlled to a large degree by white supremacy. Schools, churches, so-cial clubs, businesses, and courts were run by and for white folk. The point of politics was to defend white interests.

Politicians did not have to name white interests because they were considered American interests. The founders and the original citizens made white-ness the default position of American identity and hu-manity. American citizens were allowed to be white without having to say so. They could rely on the bene-fits of whiteness without having to name them—one of which was the celebration that attended the notion of the self-made man. It was an identity that gave white folk a false sense of achievement by connecting them to an ancestry whose claims to glory rested on the lie of their own hard work—work that had instead been outsourced to enslaved black folk.

White politicians took office to maintain the status quo well into the twentieth century. Racist and xeno-phobic figures were only portrayed as out of step once civil rights leaders and other black activists challenged their politics and the society that would elect them.

Racial progress forced an adjustment in the means of propagating the idea that America is a white society. Dixiecrats like George Wallace maintained the earlier political consensus of white superiority. Later politicians were conflicted: they were lodged between the unspoken endorsement of white supremacy and the effort to do away with old-style politics. The strategy of some white politicians was to accept existing racial politics to get elected and then use their position to remedy the most troubling aspects of the racial order. It was a risky bargain, and one that often left black folk in the lurch. Lyndon Baines Johnson pulled it off to perfection when he managed to pass the holy trinity of civil rights legislation: the 1964 Civil Rights Act, the 1965 Voting Rights Act, and the 1968 Fair Housing Act. If LBJ is the gold standard, then John F. Kennedy was far less glorious in his fatal hesitancies about civil rights as president. His brother Bobby is sandwiched between the two, lauded for the scope of his aspiration near the end of his life and yet lacking the broad political measure of his promise.

President Kennedy was a northern white liberal who subscribed to the idea of equality in the abstract without endorsing a revolutionary overhaul of racial politics. He got a big boost in black communities because of a symbolic gesture—as a presidential candidate, the Massachusetts senator placed a telephone call to Georgia's governor, Ernest Vandiver, to get

Martin Luther King out of jail in October 1960, right before the election that put Kennedy in the Oval Office.[2] While the gesture endeared him to black folk, Kennedy was careful not to alienate his white supporters. Kennedy had infamously courted white southern voters by meeting with their leaders to reassure them he would not be a vigilant advocate of civil rights. Kennedy pledged to Vandiver that as president he would never use federal authority to coerce school desegregation in Georgia. In office, President Kennedy put conservative bigots on the federal court; recoiled at the sight of the interracially married entertainer Sammy Davis, Jr., when he appeared with his wife, Mai Britt, at a White House celebration of Abraham Lincoln's birthday; and attempted to string King and other black leaders along as much as possible. His equivocations and vacillations amounted to precious little for black folk. President Kennedy gained a greater reputation for civil rights support in death than he had earned in life.[3]

Bobby, if not quite his brother's opposite, was at least his sometime foil: he knew less about civil rights than Jack, yet he hungered more to make a difference. On that day in New York, in that room, it all came to a head. When Bobby confronted Baldwin and his confreres, he presumed the legitimacy of politics in a way that may have worked for King, but surely not for Baldwin, ever the skeptic of white power. King was committed to working within the parameters of political legitimacy. Baldwin and some of his mates doubted the will of the state to reconcile itself to black destiny.

Baldwin could more easily acknowledge his doubts because he wasn't in the same position as King, Roy Wilkins, Whitney Young, and other black leaders. Their raison d'être was to uphold the state as the bulwark against black suffering. But Baldwin questioned the intent of the state because it had collapsed into—become identical with—whiteness. King understood white supremacy as a distortion of democracy, as an interruption of the delivery of social goods. Thus, his "I Have a Dream" speech suggested that the American Dream was sufficient to accommodate the aspirations of black folk. The adjustment had to be made in society's laws, customs, habits, traditions, and conventions. Baldwin believed the state was doing exactly what it was set up to do: undermine blackness. Thus, black animus was a condition of the state's very existence. Recognition of blackness was an aberration, a failure of the system, a weakness.

When Bobby butted heads with Jerome Smith over patriotism, Bobby was proclaiming his vision of the state as a bulwark of protection of its citizens, who, in exchange, repay the state with their loyalty. Their mutual adherence rests on the belief that the best interests of the citizen are realized through the state, and the state's true existence is measured in the loyalty of its citizens. When Smith protested that he had no interest in defending his country, Bobby took that as a sign of utter disrespect. What he failed to see was that Smith and other black folk had already endured the gravest form of disrespect possible: the denial of active citizenship and the rich realization of American identity with a full complement of rights. Although he thought of himself as empathetic to black folk, Kennedy was acting from the basis of projection: he cast onto Smith and the other blacks the notion that what he was, they could be. That is why Bobby easily asserted that his immigrant family was the perfect example of how black folk could be absorbed and supported by the state.

Baldwin knew that tinkering with public policy was of little use if the value of black life had not been established. That's why he and his fellow blacks spent so much time insisting on being heard and, most important, seen. The dual meaning of *witness* becomes clear: Baldwin as witness, and Baldwin being witnessed, being seen. Baldwin as witness brought the full panoply of his gifts to bear. His voice was a weapon of witness.

Optics are critical in discussing politics and race. Who is seen and witnessed as important gets the spoils. When Baldwin and his friends spoke, their speech may have been dismissed as merely emotional, but it was so much more: it was the data of the internal dimensions of racial experience; it was blackness seen through the prism of pain and trauma; it was knowledge rooted in black priorities—what an experience means, how it registers, and what effect it has on the black body. That is why Smith's witness was so compelling: it was the knowledge his body brought, the knowledge rooted in the hardship he endured. It was more than a problem of knowledge; it was an ethical question, too, a problem of how whites could morally accommodate the knowledge his suffering brought, and what it implied about the immoral character of white society.

* * *

A different kind of challenge loomed when a black president was elected: How, and to what degree, would experience and witness play into policy? What was the quality and nature of his experience as a black man, how would it shape his understanding of his role and job, and how would it add, or subtract, from his duties? Would his blackness constitute an existential weight, a knowledge of suffering, and also one of possibility, and thus color his views of democracy and shape his approach to making laws?

For the first time, a black face was on the machinery that had worked hard to undermine black agency. But a black face in a high place does not guarantee a new order. Obama offered the state legitimacy more than he offered black folk inclusion. One black face could not possibly overcome the historic legacy of black erasure. Obama was a walking legitimation crisis, throwing into conniptions the very state he represented because it meant, by implication, or extension, that the blacks it had historically demeaned and excluded were now part of official American identity, were that much closer to being perceived as full citizens. And so an equally powerful wind blew back, insisting that Obama could never be truly American, truly a citizen, truly the symbol of the nation as its putative father because he was, in essence, illegitimate, a bastard president, a political orphan with no lines of kinship to authentic American identity. No matter, or amount, of policy can solve that.

Obama's blackness, no matter how curtailed, made him, even as president, an enemy of the state. The white refusal to concede Obama's legitimacy was the articulation of the deeply rooted refusal to see blackness as American. Donald Trump's birtherism was the extended unfolding of such an idea. For those who take solace in the belief that Trump is a marginal player in whiteness, they are sadly mistaken. He is, indeed, the extension of the logic of American ideas about blackness found at the nation's roots and beginnings. Baldwin and friends understood the roots of whiteness as the determinant of our politics before King could acknowledge it.[4] It is true that Malcolm X and the black nationalists were capable of seeing this, but their handicap was twofold: first, they didn't get involved in electoral politics; and second, they bathed in a politics of racial resentment that matched whiteness in spirit. That is why Malcolm could meet with white supremacists from the Nazi Party, like George Lincoln Rockwell, in 1961 to map out their mutual strategies for racial separation. For all of its ferocity of black self-love, there was about Malcolm's position a galling naïveté about how such things operated in the real world of politics. The black nationalists' belief that they and white supremacists wanted the same thing was fatally ignorant.

Recently, as bigotry resurfaces, symbolized in the events in Charlottesville in August 2017, the lie is put to the belief that "this is not American, this is not us," when, indeed, it truly is. We do not want to acknowledge how true it is because it makes us look complicit in prejudice we thought we had gotten over. Donald Trump is far more representative of the nation than many whites would like to admit.

But there is a development with Trump that is unique: he is treating the nation—which, by default, is white and Christian, though technically it is neither— as white folk have treated black folk throughout our history. Trump is treating the entire nation as black. More particularly, he is treating the entire nation as "the nigger." One of the reasons for the special outrage of many white Americans toward him is that he has forgotten the rules; that sort of treatment is for blacks, not whites. That need not be a conscious belief for it to be true. The reason his views on immigration can be abided is because those immigrants are "them." However, when it comes to insulting folk, spoiling his office in narcissistic displays, acting vengefully—this is the heart of whiteness, and the force of whiteness against blackness and other colors. It has always been a rather juvenile affair: drinking at a white water fountain was not simply a marker of rigid, though unscientific, anthropology, it was the symbolic height of adolescent bravura and competition—mine is better than yours. Except such displays are rigged from the start to favor petulant whiteness. It is unbearable to white America for Donald Trump to treat "them" like "they" treated "us." In short, he's confused his pronouns. If they could abide the language and grasp the comparison, many whites would cry out with James Baldwin: "I am not your nigger."

After a great deal of resistance, combat, and protest, some white folk have come around to seeing race, especially this brand of whiteness, as a fiction, something Baldwin said more than 50 years ago. Many whites now see the truth because they believe that what Trump is doing is deeply and profoundly flawed, even lunatic. His obsessions and perverse preoccupations are the stuff of a whiteness that never had

to be held accountable. Trump's total lack of knowledge, and the enshrinement of ignorance as the basis
of power and authority, is the personification of white
supremacy and white arrogance.

Obama and Trump are thus wedged between two
poles of unbelievability: that Obama, the ultimate
"traitor" to American identity, could be elected; and
that Trump could recklessly give away the family se-
crets by exposing the twisted logic of whiteness for
the world to see. It is unthinkable to many whites that
such a man could be president, that such a figure, with
his array of flaws, could take command. After all, a
subtler, or more sophisticated, whiteness often occu-
pies the presidency. But the truth is that Trump har-
kens back to original and founding whiteness.

Even before he took office Donald Trump was
plagued by a chronic ignorance of black life, an ignorance spiked by a mean-spirited incuriosity about
even the fundamental facts of black existence, a pose
amplified in the Oval Office as he addressed Frederick
Douglass as if he were alive and starring as the second
baseman for the Baltimore Orioles. Trump argued on
the campaign trail that "African-American communities are absolutely in the worst shape they've ever been
in before. Ever, ever, ever."[5] President Barack Obama
drolly declared, "I mean, he missed that whole civics
lesson about slavery or Jim Crow."[6]

Trump's ignorance about race, his critical lack of
nuance and learning about it, is disheartening enough.

But it prevails among liberals and the white left, too, in their 2016 post-election calls to forego identity politics. If there is a dirty secret in American life it is this: the real unifying force in our national cultural and political life, beyond skirmishes over ideology and party, is white identity masked as universal, neutral, and therefore quintessentially American. The greatest purveyors of identity politics today, and for the bulk of our country's history, have been white citizens. This means that among the oldest forms of "fake news" in the nation's long trek to democratic opportunity has been the belief that whiteness is identical to the idea of what it means to be American.

Senator Bernie Sanders, despite his dramatically different politics and ideology, is, in many ways, the mirror image of Donald Trump: a brash, older white male with professed sympathies for the white working class and little knowledge of black folk. From the start of his 2016 presidential campaign, Sanders was prickly about race, uncomfortable with an outspoken, demanding blackness, resistant to letting go of his preference for class over race, or really, of subsuming race under class. Though he made efforts to correct his poor racial sight, Sanders remained at heart a man of the people, especially if those people were white working-class folk. After the election, Sanders sounded an increasingly familiar theme among liberals that they should "go beyond identity politics." Sanders warned that "to think of diversity purely in racial and gender terms is not sufficient," and that we need candidates "to be fighters for the working class and stand up to the corporate powers who have so much power over our economic lives." In a speech in November 2016 in California, Sanders said that it is "very easy for many Americans to say, I hate racism, I hate homophobia, I hate sexism," but that "it is a little bit harder for people in the middle or upper middle class to say, maybe we do have to deal with the greed of Wall Street."[7]

This is a nifty bit of historical revisionism. For the longest time there was little consideration for diversity, even among liberal elites, much less the white middle and working classes. Diversity was calculated in terms of region, sometimes religion, or vocation, as long as everyone involved was white. Race and gender, and sexuality too, were late to the game. It seems more than a little reactionary to blame the loss of the election on a brand of identity politics that even liberals were slow to embrace, and that not all of them are completely sold on. Moreover, Sanders, like so many liberals and progressives, spurns the very diversity that gave the ideals of democracy legs. It is not that attention to diversity and identity somehow undercuts our nation's embrace of democratic goals; it strengthens them. The black struggle for freedom has ensured that other groups could follow along in the wake of our demand for equality.

When the 1964 civil rights bill was in doubt in Congress, crafty and bigoted white representatives thought they could sink it by attaching the issue of gender, hoping to appeal to the sexism of those who might otherwise be cajoled to offer their support. Instead the bill passed and paved the way both for black rights and, with Title VII, those of women. What's good for black folk is good for the nation. It is more than a little curious that, in the name of a mythical universalism stripped of race, gender, or sexuality, advocates across the political spectrum now advance a nation of populist anti-identity politics driven by a vigorous defense of identity as they laud the white working class. It is not that the white working class is unworthy of serious attention and broad support. It is that their fortunes are cast over and against the masses of folk of color, many of whom are also working class or poor, but whose interests hardly factor into considerations of class consciousness, class rebellion, or class solidarity.

* * *

To accept the framework advanced by Trump and Sanders, we must be resolutely ahistorical. The interests of the white working class have often been used by white political elites to stave off challenges to inequality and discrimination by black folk and other minority groups. First, in the early twentieth century, the rights of black folk were denied because they would undermine white working-class stability. Then, in the various worker unions in the middle part of the twentieth century, black agency and mobility were curtailed so as to protect the interests of white work-ing- and middle-class folk. In the late sixties, Richard Nixon even supported a version of affirmative action because he deemed it useful to break unions by ac-cusing them of racial exclusion. In the eighties Ron-ald Reagan appealed to disaffected white Democrats who resented being forced to share a small measure of the enormous gains they had accumulated through bigotry and official discrimination. And now we hear again the hue and cry that the neglected white work-ing class was the linchpin to the 2016 election and is the future of American progressive politics. The more things change, the more they stay the same.

The truth is that American politics has hardly ne-glected the interests of the white working and middle classes. The progress experienced under the banner of the movement for racial, gender, and sexual jus-tice has forced white folk to share just a little of their bounty with blacks, Latinos, women, and queer folk. To be sure, these groups are hardly homogenous or univocal. Yet concern for their own interests leads whites to think of their well being at the expense of other groups, compromising the nation's democratic health. Instead, there is talk of restoring America to a nostalgic vision of white dominance under Donald Trump, or, in progressive circles, to a mythological, coherent, homogenized group that lacks the plagues of identity politics. But identity has always been at the heart of American culture. We must confront a truth that we have assiduously avoided: the most protected, cherished, and nurtured identity of all has been white identity.

That whiteness is the nation's preferred identity becomes painfully obvious when white bigots scamper out of their closets at the first sign of support from our government. It is difficult to argue that the ugly bigotry unleashed in 2017 in the streets of Charlottesville, Virginia—when white supremacists and Neo-Nazis rallied in a "Unite the Right" march to protest the removal of statues of Confederate generals from city parks, resulting in the death of valiant anti–white supremacist protester Heather D. Heyer—had nothing to do with the election of Donald Trump, one of the whitest presidents, with one of the whitest administrations, in the history of this nation. White separatist David Duke declared that the alt-right unity fiasco "fulfills the promises of Donald Trump." Trump infamously offered false equivalencies between white bigots and their protesters by suggesting that there were "some very fine people on both sides."[8]

The ungainly assembly of white supremacists in Charlottesville trampled on the facts of political history with a willfully distorted version of the past. Their resentment of the removal of public symbols of the Confederate past is fueled by revisionist history on steroids. These whites fancy themselves the victims of the so-called politically correct assault on American democracy, a perception that propelled Trump to victory. Together, Trump and white nationalists constitute the repulsive resurgence of a virulent *bigotocracy,* a loosely organized confederate of white racists who seek to institutionalize their ideology as national habit, social custom, cultural convention, and, when possible, legal bulwark. Trump and the white bigotocracy have little patience for real history. If there's one word that calls whiteness to account, if there's a single phrase that conjures all the heartbreak that bigotry created and that blacks have endured, that word is slavery. White bigots think black folk have pimped that term for far too long, lived too long on the memory of something that happened so long ago that it can't possibly have anything to do with what's going on today.

Of course, the bigotocracy ignores how the destiny of the black folk bigots despise is tied to the history and destiny of white America. It overlooks fundamental facts about slavery in this country: that blacks were stolen from their African homeland to toil for no wages in American dirt and turn it into cotton and gold. When black folk and others point that out, it grieves white bigots. They are especially offended when it is argued that slavery changed its clothes during Reconstruction, dressing up as freedom only to keep menacing black folk as it did during Jim Crow. The bigotocracy is angry that slavery is seen as this nation's original sin; they cling for life to a faded southern aristocracy whose benefits—of moral and intellectual supremacy—trickled down to ordinary whites. If they couldn't drink from the cup of economic advantage, they could sip what was left of such a hateful ideology in the belief that at least they weren't black. The renowned scholar W.E.B. Du Bois called this alleged sense of superiority the "psychological wage" of whiteness. President Lyndon Baines Johnson once argued, "If you can convince the lowest white man he's better than the best colored man, he won't notice you're picking his pocket. Hell, give him somebody to look down on, and he'll empty his pockets for you."[9]

It is disheartening for black folk to see such a vile and despicable replay of history before our very eyes. It is depressing to realize that what we confronted as children may yet be the legacy we bequeath to our children as well. It is more dispiriting still to realize that the government of our land, at least in the present administration, has shown little empathy for victims of white bigotry and, indeed, has helped to spread the paralyzing virus of black hatred, as much by turning a deaf ear and blind eye as by actively encouraging a fretful gaggle of hatemongers. Nothing could more clearly declare the moral bankruptcy of our country.

There is little hope that the Trump administration will give a quarter in the fight for the nation's democratic legacy as it deepens the stakes of white supremacy through memory warfare and a nostalgia that masks political failure and historical distortion. One of the most notable symbols of the Trump administration's troubling strategy is the insistence by Chief of Staff John Kelly that "the lack of an ability to compromise led to the Civil War." Kelly said that the Civil War was fought between "men and women of good faith on both sides," including the "honorable" Robert E. Lee.[10] The left duly excoriated Kelly for his willful neglect of history—after all, there could be little compromise with a Confederacy and its star general out to subjugate black folk no matter the cost. But in Kelly's defense it was noted that the source of his rumination was none other than the Ken Burns *Civil War* documentary that featured the prolific commentary of novelist and southern historian Shelby Foote. That Kelly echoed Foote was a neat trick of ideological ventriloquism: the right got its views endorsed in a widely celebrated masterpiece of documentary filmmaking by a figure whose liberal bona fides are unquestioned. Burns offered Foote wide latitude in expounding his view that Lee and the Confederacy had other fish to fry than enslavement, and that the war was fueled by the failure of the North and South to compromise. This is historical revision at its worst. When we engage Foote's work off-screen it is more complicated, but, alas, more troubling still.

When it comes to slavery and the Civil War, Foote rose to poetry to describe the intramural tragedies that stabbed the American breast. He knew the facts of chattel slavery and the realities of subjugation. But he missed the truth of just how intertwined with the American soul was the greatest war we fought to clarify our national destiny. Shelby Foote's view that Lincoln injected slavery as an issue into the Civil War to gain tactical advantage over the South is dangerously close to the idea that all that bloodshed was more about states' rights than about whether we should continue to shackle black humanity. Foote's Civil War trilogy unabashedly tilted toward the Confederacy and can be read as a monumental brief on behalf of the Southern view of the Late Unpleasantness. Foote was upended by the racial traditions from which he sprang and from which he derived his sense of history, one that steadfastly denied the prominent place of race from the start in the War Between the States. Years later, Foote said that he could understand the consternation of black folk around the Confederate flag—while concluding they hadn't got it right. After denouncing the "knotheads down home—the Ku Kluxers and the rest of them," Foote said: "I know that flag really pains black people. It was used against them in a dastardly way, and they hate it. And I understand their hating it. But they are wrong."[11] If only his admirers could be half as honest.

Bobby Kennedy said in the early '60s that he would have gone to the Mississippi Delta to work for the Negro if he hadn't gone into politics, and that shamed Foote into a recognition that, had it been applied to his trilogy, may have made a substantive difference in his telling of the story.

> And it hurt me to think that I had turned my back on something that Bobby Kennedy had been willing to devote his whole life to. You grow up in a thing and you're not inclined to see the evil as clearly as you would if you were visiting that place. It seems so much a part and parcel of the life, especially when it contributes to your comfort, as it did to mine. The race question is the big thing.[12]

Race *is* the big thing, and Foote's acknowledgment of its role in national life should be the starting place for any history of the Civil War—and not just that war, but the bigger war, the war for the soul of a nation that needs far more Bobby Kennedys willing to confront the catastrophe of their ignorance and far fewer Donald Trumps sworn to hold their bigotry sacred and to enshrine their vengeful unenlightenment as knowledge.

* * *

What Baldwin and his crew exposed in that room continues to resonate with us today. The "other" is the fuel that drives ideas of American society, that feeds American identity. If we are committed to discerning, then defeating, the contemporary logic of racism, we must separate it from its ties to democracy itself. In order to be true patriots, we must become disloyal to chronically prejudiced views of American society that persist in our rather ignoble Trumpian moment. We earn the politicians we deserve, inherit the systems we admire and find useful, no matter our protests to the contrary. Are there any politicians on the horizon who will tell the truth and understand our reluctance to be honest about race? Is there a witness?

"I think part of the reason is slavery," California senator Kamala Harris tells me. "And you can't talk about the history of race in America without talking about slavery. It's the sin, the blemish, a shameful part of our history. To talk about race in America requires one to face truth in terms of the disparities that exist based on race. And the truth makes people very uncomfortable. There's a natural desire to have conversations where everyone walks away feeling lovely, and it's been pleasant. But not so much when you're talking about race."

In our day, politicians who tell the truth seem increasingly, and depressingly, rare. Harris says that the act of witness has not yet exhausted its usefulness.

"I think one of the most significant developments in the fight for civil rights in this country was the creation and invention of the smartphone. Because for the first time white people could actually *see* and *witness* for themselves what was going on."

Harris believes that colonialism provides a perfect example of how racism and cultural blindness conspire to prevent a reckoning with our complicity in oppression. "Colonialists think they discovered something because they're seeing it for the first time. No! This has *been* going on. There are communities that have been experiencing this for generations and generations. But you're seeing it for the first time, and now you're aware of it. And I think that the Black Lives Matter Movement was about young people rising up in an environment that has allowed us to elevate and amplify certain conversations. Because the subject of that conversation has become much more apparent. And so, on an issue like bias in policing, or excessive force, or racial profiling, technology allowed that conversation to actually occur with a much broader group of people. And because of the way that folks are organizing with technology, it is reminiscent of what my parents did in the sixties."

Harris acknowledges the crucial importance of the optics of race. "We, as leaders, do everything we can to amplify and lift up the voices of the community. There's an expression in many African countries when you meet somebody for the first time. The greeting is not 'Pleased to meet you.' The greeting is 'I see you.' And I see you in all of the dimensions of who you are. I see you in full relief. I see you based on the complexity of your life, like everyone else's life. And I think that part of it is that we, in lifting up the community, have to require that everyone understands the complexity, or sees the community in full relief. And understanding then that if you're talking with a black woman, you should understand it's a black woman's issue. The economy is a black woman's issue. Education is a black woman's issue. Health-care reform is a black woman's issue. Combating climate change is a black woman's issue. Black Lives Matter is a black woman's issue. People talk now about intersectionality. That relates to the various forms that one identifies with, or identifies themselves as being. But I would say that, as leaders, we have to understand that no one constituency is a monolith."

Harris argues that courage in the face of hate is our only option.

> The forces that are sowing hate and division
> are stronger than they've been in a long time.
> And so how do we deal with it? Well, one, we
> don't cower. And instead we rededicate to
> making sure our voices are loud and strong
> and unified. We reject the notion that we're a
> divided America. We reject the notion that it's
> "us versus them." I think we're having conver-
> sations across the board that we have put off
> or have not had, or need to have. And we must
> speak the truth. Racism is real in this country.
> Sexism is real in this country. Homophobia is
> real in this country. Anti-Semitism is real in
> this country. The anti-Muslim anti-immigrant
> sentiment is real in this country. And this is a
> moment that is requiring all of us to acknowl-
> edge those hard but real truths.

Only when we have a full-throated voicing of our vibrant democracy in all of its splendidly cantanker-ous diversity can we truly claim at last to be American. One of Robert Kennedy's grandsons, Joseph Kennedy, a congressman from Massachusetts, understands the need for such diversity. Called upon by the Democrats to respond to Donald Trump's first State of the Union address, Kennedy, in his first nationally televised speech, underscored his belief in progressive poli-tics and empathy for working-class folk and people of color that characterized the views of his grandfather.

"We see an economy that makes stocks soar, investor portfolios bulge, and corporate profits climb, but fails to give workers their fair share," Kennedy said. "An all-out war on environmental protection. A Justice Department rolling back civil rights by the day. Hatred and supremacy proudly marching in our streets."

Kennedy argued that partisanship and political differences alone can't explain the chaos the nation endures because of the Trump presidency. "This administration isn't just targeting the laws that protect us; they are targeting the very idea that we are all worthy of protection." Kennedy, like Harris, struck at the homophobia, xenophobia, racism, and anti-Muslim fervor gripping the nation and finding amplification in the White House. "For them, dignity isn't something you're born with but something you measure, by . . . the gender of your spouse, the country of your birth, the color of your skin, the God of your prayers." Harkening, perhaps, to the time 50 years ago when his grandfather famously visited the Appalachian poor, Kennedy spoke of the false choices the administration forces on us: "coal miners or single moms, rural communities or inner cities, the coast or the heartland" are not "bitter rivals" but "rather mutual casualties of a system forcefully rigged towards those at the top."

In contrast to the conservative embrace of big business and the rich, Kennedy said that Democrats "choose a living wage, and paid leave, and affordable child care . . . pensions that are solvent, trade pacts that are fair, roads and bridges that won't rust away, a good education that you can afford." Kennedy showed flashes of his great-uncle John Kennedy's eloquence, too, when he declared:

> That is our story. It began the day our founding fathers and mothers set sail for a new world, fleeing oppression and intolerance. It continued with every word of our independence, the audacity to declare that all men are created equal, an imperfect promise for a nation struggling to become a more perfect union. It grew with every suffragette's step, every Freedom Rider's voice, and every weary soul we welcomed to our shores.[13]

Kennedy spoke directly to the Dreamers in Spanish when he said, "Usteded son parte de nuestra historia. Vamos a luchar. Vamos a luchar por estedes y no nos vamos alejar. [You are part of our story. We will fight for you. And we will not walk away.]" Kennedy nodded as well to the #MeToo and Black Lives Matter movements, both founded by black women. In referencing Trump without mentioning his name, Kennedy assured his listeners that bullies "may land a punch," that they "may leave a mark," but that "they have never—not once in the history of the United States—managed to match the strength and spirit of people united in defense of their future."

Yet, as with Harris and all politicians, their worth and mettle can only be tested and assured when they are challenged to do their best. And no matter their race, gender, or sexual orientation, politicians must strive to represent the full range of citizens in order to realize true democracy for all.

That has certainly been true for Minneapolis city councilwoman Andrea Jenkins, the first black openly transgender woman elected to public office in the United States. Jenkins believes that politicians have a duty to channel activism into public policy.

> At this particular moment in American history, and with this democratic structure that we set up, the role of a politician, and even more specifically a black politician, is to harness the power of all of this activism that's happening, and then make policies to address it. Because it's amazing to lay out on the freeway and stop traffic. But that doesn't necessarily create the change. That creates the opportunity for the change. But that can't be our only tactic. We've got to use the electoral process to make the changes that address the challenges that people are bringing forward.

Jenkins has thought long and hard about how policies should not simply help folk in theory, but should effectively transform their existence because the policies concretely and realistically address actual needs.

> When I say representation matters, I think people from those [vulnerable] communities are going to be looking at not only how [this] can help people, but also what might be some of the unintended consequences of these policy decisions that we're making. And make sure that we are not creating more problems than we are solving. So, for example, fifteen dollars minimum wage sounds beautiful. On its face it's an amazing thing to make these corporations pay at least the bare minimum value of our labor. But when [workers'] salaries go up, they're going to become ineligible for medical assistance for their kids, and SNAP, that supplements their income with food. That's an unintended consequence. And frankly, fifteen dollars an hour is not even nearly going to make up for that. So how do you mitigate that? And I think that's the importance of having, in our representative government, people that represent every part of our community and look beyond surface benefits and try to figure out negative impacts as well.

Jenkins proudly calls on her background as a writer and performance artist to inspire her constituency and to draw parallels between the artistic enterprise and the political effort to bring social change.

> I'm a poet. I'm a true hip-hop head, which I believe [sparks an] absolutely prophetic message in black American struggle because it has incorporated all of the expressive forms of the last two centuries, from gospel to jazz to R&B, the blues, as well as this whole pop phenomenon that has taken place in the last fifty years. It has been able to speak to the struggles of black people in ways that have never been done before. And I promised myself that I'm not giving up my art for this political thing. So, I might read a poem from the dais. And that's how you bring that pain, bring that suffering. And the real bottom line is, nothing has really changed. [Injustice] is still happening today. So it's not like we're just trying to redress grievances from the past. We're trying to stop you from harming us right now.

Jenkins believes in an intersectional politics, and a broadly humane and inclusive one, too.

> I just try to model my life as one who is working to improve humanity. And that includes making life better for Barron Trump. If we lived in a world that had full health care for everybody,

and full employment for everybody, no sexual harassment, no unequal pay for women, access to safe and affordable housing, I'm pretty sure life would be better for Barron too. And we'd be trying to speak up for those issues and always making sure to be inclusive, modeling the behavior that disabled lives matter, and women's lives matter. LGBT people's lives matter. Black lives matter. And showing people that in real and authentic ways.

Jenkins believes that her pioneering work as a transgender politician augurs well for progressive politics across the land.

I've been out here for a long time, but there are also a lot of young folks. You see what [transgender author and activist] Janet Mock is doing, and [transgender actress] Laverne Cox. They're making moves. I will point out that I was out and being active and working for their freedom when they were in grade school! But I love them and I'm proud of them. So I don't think it's just me. In fact, I think there's like eighty-something trans people running for office in 2018. Clearly not all of them are going to win. But some of them are. And I think that my election, along with six other trans people that were elected last year, has inspired a lot of people. And not just transgender people. I've got so many sisters up here running for office, telling me they are running because I won. And I don't know if I should take that as a compliment, or [if they're thinking] "Damn, if this black trans girl can run, I know I can win." But you know what? If they are thinking that, so be it. They're discounting the fact that I worked very hard on my campaign. We raised more money than anybody ever running for this seat has ever raised. We increased voter turnout by 11%. I won by 73%. So that means my volunteers were out there. I had young people working on my campaign—young women, in fact. My campaign manager was a twenty-one-year-old Pakistani girl, still in college. I'm glad that they're inspired. I think [my victory] will have some positive reverb in the future.

While Jenkins believes that the issues impacting trans communities are important to address, it is equally important to wrestle with the issues affecting a broad array of minority and oppressed constituencies.

"I don't think we can afford to be in a silo and make progress . . . There would be no gay liberation movement if there wasn't a civil rights movement. And the women's rights movement too. So they all build on each other because they're all interrelated. I think the biggest enemy, and the biggest oppression, in my mind, in all of this, is white supremacy, patriarchy, which is closely related to sexism and religious subjugation, and if you get at all of that, all these other issues get resolved." Jenkins' fierce commitment to a broad vision of democracy rests on telling the truth and directing political resources to help our nation's most vulnerable and traumatized members.

If American politics is to regain its juice, recapture its vigor, it must be pushed and shaped by vibrant figures who hold it accountable. When Baldwin and his friends confronted Bobby Kennedy, Kennedy got mad, but then anger gave way to honest reflection and sincere self-criticism. Bobby had to reckon with the invisibility of black humanity, even to his own liberal eyes, especially his own privileged eyes. But in that abrasive exchange with Baldwin and his friends, enough humanity seeped through to let him at least hear the echoes of their trauma. And in that moment there was emotional movement on his part, if not full-blown transformation.

THE ARTISTS

Black artists have rarely, if ever, enjoyed the luxury of making work that is divorced from black culture. The political situation of black folk in this country—we are not the majority, our social vulnerabilities wear on us, our existence still provokes wonder and fear—means that our creations will inevitably be viewed through the lens of race. Black artwork always represents more than the work we are looking at, more than the purpose or vision that governs its creation. When Baldwin spoke of the "burden of representation," each term in the phrase did its work. The burden for a black artist is how to tell the truth while also representing *us,* and whatever "we" the artist happens to claim, which amounts to the version of blackness she chooses to embrace or defend. Pitfalls abound for the black artist: Does she avoid politics and stick to "pure" art, if that is even possible, only paying heed to the howl of authenticity from her own soul? Or is the black artist's creation a pledge of fealty to the group from which she emerges, a repayment of sorts for the inspiration to think or write or speak or see as she does?

The black artists gathered in that room certainly felt a compulsion to set the record straight about a blackness that had forever been savaged by stereotype or stultified by white liberal validation. Authentic blackness rarely got the chance to just breathe, to live in its own skin and walk at its own pace. Blackness was hostage to white envy or evisceration. It was liked or loathed, misunderstood, explained, underappreciated, fought over, fought against, detested, elevated, emptied of its dangerous otherness. And yet it was prized for just that reason, that, in the jarring contrast to sterile whiteness, it might conjure a bewildering, even alluring blackness, a blackness that offered the illusion of beastly wildness yet was as tame as white culture needed it to be. The challenge of the black artist was to wrestle white folk for the meaning of blackness.

Black art was at once an argument about black intelligence and black humanity, the presumed lack of which set the basis for understanding the fatal deficiencies of black life. Black folk could never match the intellectual pedigree of their European counterparts;

they could never master the sophisticated expression and abstract reasoning of their noble white peers. Black folk were neither smart, nor human, nor, therefore, capable of producing true art. Of course, black art forgot to take note of objections to its existence. The answer of black art was, by virtue of its excellence, to win a hearing in a white world that doubted its truth and reality. Or to damn the white world to its own perdition while enjoying its own artistic paradise.

Black art couldn't help but be political as its creation rebutted a philosophy that doubted its existence. The very notion that black folk could be capable of art challenged Western ideas about what black folk are good at and what we should be expected to produce or understand. Thomas Jefferson doubted the ability of the Negro to pursue refined knowledge. Even when we proved we could do so, when, for instance, Phillis Wheatley grasped poetic meter and displayed a mastery of Greek that was said to be the proof of intelligence, there was always an asterisk, an insistence that we were not quite up to snuff, that we were hopelessly inferior.[1] Black art could at once satisfy the urge to create and validate the worth of black culture. There could never be art for its own sake. That's because the sake that art existed for had been purchased with the blood of the oppressed. Their forced labor and physical sacrifice made it possible for those whites who were free to produce and appreciate art.

James Baldwin had embraced a blackness that was willful, joyous, even riotous in its self-expression and saw no need to ask whites for permission to exist. He argued that the artist must embrace the very thing most folk avoid: the aloneness of the human condition. Part of what it means to be human is to wrestle with the aloneness of "birth, suffering, love, and death"; the artist must encourage folk to engage what they would rather avoid, to "correct the delusions to which we fall prey in our attempts to avoid this knowledge." For Baldwin, the artist is the ultimate "disturber of the peace." Cultivating aloneness undoubtedly, at times, puts the artist at odds with the culture from which he sprang. The black artist must speak for himself if he is to also speak for the broader community. Earlier in his career, Baldwin was leery of reducing art to propaganda, or to the expression of group interests, since, as he said, "literature and sociology are not one and the same."[2]

But Baldwin eventually concluded that it is possible to be true to one's individual imperatives while echoing the vision of others, as "it is the writer's necessity to deal as truthfully as possible with his own experience, and it is his hope to enlarge his experience to contain the experience of others, of millions."[3] Artists have a dual function: first, they know the truth of the human condition. Second, artists prove, and help humanity to grapple with, the notion that "safety is an illusion," thus "all artists are divorced from and even necessarily opposed to any system whatever." One might think that Baldwin's subsequent career contradicted this sentiment since his art supported the black freedom struggle. Yet it was his independence and outsider status as a queer man, and having one foot in and the other foot outside the nonviolent movement for social change, that made him a wildcard. It may even have kept him from the speaker's rostrum at the March on Washington.

Baldwin resisted being cast as the spokesman for America's Negro, but, poetically enough, it was his literary gifts that forged his place as witness to the humanity of black folk and the artifice of color. Baldwin relentlessly deconstructed the heart of whiteness.

A radical actor and singer, Harry Belafonte was also determined to use art to express and inspire a liberated imagination. Belafonte was an eager apprentice to progressives who insisted that art support black humanity and combat white supremacy long before he famously forged a relationship with Martin Luther King, Jr. Belafonte came of age in a post-war era when there was fierce debate about who or what was truly American. Many conservatives embraced narrow visions of national identity and harbored a Cold War suspicion of progressive figures and ideas. The rabid anticommunist Senator Joseph McCarthy led the way. The blacklisting of left-wing talent, especially in

Hollywood, meant that American art was hostage to a fatally limited politics of citizenship that cast free-thinking artists as traitors to the nation. The collapse of art into pro-American propaganda impoverished self-expression on stage and on the big and small screens.[4]

Belafonte found an uplifting mentor, and a cautionary tale, in Paul Robeson, the polymath whose prodigious talents and fearless pursuit of artistic freedom and social justice made him a target of McCarthy's totalitarian fantasy. Robeson was an outspoken critic of American empire who used his perch as a world-class entertainer on stage and screen to criticize racism at home and colonialism and imperialism abroad. When four black folk were killed in a mass lynching in 1946, Robeson met with President Harry Truman and warned him that if no legislation was enacted to end lynching then Negroes would defend themselves. Truman abruptly ended the meeting, stating that it was not the right time to propose anti-lynching legislation.

Robeson also worked tirelessly with trade union and civil rights groups to bolster the standing of working-class folk and black citizens. He linked their struggles to highlight the common core of oppression that each endured. In a 1949 speech before the Paris Peace Congress, Robeson argued that "We in America do not forget that it was on the backs of the white workers from Europe and on the backs of millions of Blacks that the wealth of America was built. And we resolve to share it equally." In the same speech, Robeson made his anti–Cold War position plain. "We shall not make war on anyone. We shall not make war on the Soviet Union . . . We oppose those who wish to build up imperialist Germany and to establish fascism in Greece . . . We shall support peace and friendship among all nations, with Soviet Russia and the people's Republics." Shortly afterward Robeson found himself blacklisted. Robeson was for a while forbidden to travel overseas because the State Department didn't think he should air his criticism of the American treatment of black folk in foreign countries.

Robeson was summoned to appear before the House Un-American Activities Committee after refusing to sign an affidavit affirming that he was not a Communist. He testified that he chose not to stay in the Soviet Union on a recent visit, despite his support for their ideology, "because my father was a slave and my people died to build [the United States, and] I am going to stay here, and have a part of it just like you and no fascist-minded people will drive me from it." Robeson insisted that "Whether I am or am not a Communist is irrelevant. The question is whether American citizens, regardless of their political beliefs, or sympathies, may enjoy their constitutional rights." His passport was revoked and he suffered tremendous financial loss. Tragically, he was hounded into silence by the FBI. This fiercely independent black man whose stentorian voice reverberated in passionate defense of black and other vulnerable people was demonized by a government agency. Robeson ended up clinically depressed, with a host of physical ailments that left him depleted and exhausted until he died a broken and spent man at age 77 in 1976.[5]

Robeson's tragic example, just one among many, led Belafonte to disguise his radical politics by appearing to be primarily a matinee idol, a highly regarded recording star, and a television and film producer. But in choosing what songs to sing, what roles to play, and what projects to produce, Belafonte was carefully crafting a body of work that was fueled by a deep sense of responsibility to challenge racist views of black folk, to broaden the definition of black identity, and to use his gifts to rally his fellow artists and the broader world to the cause of black freedom. Belafonte took great pains, at great risk, never to separate his artistic vision from his political perspectives. He did not seek to reduce art to racial or social propaganda. Rather he pledged his moral and artistic energy to defeat the lie of white supremacy, to expose the way it dressed up its appropriation of art as the domain of the sophisticated and the elite.

The artists gathered at the Kennedy apartment strongly believed that their art ought to serve humanity, first by being excellent, and then by speaking to the day's pressing issues; they knew their gifts offered them the opportunity to represent the masses. They all wanted to help black people, and they knew that the fame their talent brought them was a valuable weapon in the war against American apartheid. Belafonte in particular was acutely aware of how the image of black folk had been distorted by Hollywood's depiction of African Americans as coons, bucks, jezebels, mammies, and dim-witted darkies. The national news media hardly did better. When it covered the horrors that black people endured, newspapers and magazines scarcely offered in-depth coverage of the deeper dimensions of black resistance. It was often left to the black artist to combat ignorance while obeying her own artistic instincts.

Belafonte actively sought to undermine the industry's complicity in shaping visual narratives of black inferiority by consciously appealing to a broader base of blackness than the industry seemed willing or able to acknowledge. Belafonte's West Indian roots, and his penchant for exploring and embracing music and ideas across the black diaspora, merged with his insistence on a global and international perspective on black freedom struggles. He saw the black quest for freedom in America as part of the liberation struggles of black and other peoples of color, and of other oppressed peoples around the world.

Belafonte repeatedly promised to never sell out black folk, to never capitulate to the production of images or sounds that threatened the dignity and humanity of black folk. He said he would never take "Uncle Tom" roles and would refuse segregated bookings; that he would not "bite his tongue when people around him, colored or white, express bigotry, narrow-mindedness, or chauvinism in any form"; and that he would combat American apartheid by highlighting the efforts of black writers and by participating in work that featured interracial casts and performances by interracial musicians. Belafonte believed passionately that sufficiently informed white folk could be of enormous help in fostering an environment of healthy black artistic expression—and in challenging the white supremacy that undercut true democracy.[6]

Belafonte knew that pop culture could deliver vital messages of social change. But he went further and leveraged his enormous fame on behalf of the material and political interests of the black masses. He not only anted up with his own resources, he upped the ante for other artists who would have to be judged by his golden standard. But Belafonte was not interested in being the only Negro, even if he was often the first to do something—the first artist, for instance, to sell a million copies of an LP with his famed 1956 album *Calypso*. Belafonte participated in rallies, joined picket lines, marched, spoke, raised funds, and untiringly gave of body and soul to stamp out white supremacy in America and around the world.

Belafonte's example has inspired a new generation of artists to use their platforms to speak up for the
vulnerable and less fortunate members of their race.

When he received a Humanitarian Award from
Black Entertainment Television, BET, in 2016, Jesse
Williams, handsome star of the long-running landmark television show *Grey's Anatomy* and widely perceived as his generation's answer to Harry Belafonte
as an artist with a strong social conscience, leaped into
public consciousness with a searing speech that captured his progressive and courageous beliefs about
race. Williams said he accepted the award on behalf
of "real organizers all over the country—the activists,
the civil rights attorneys, the struggling parents, the
families, the teachers, the students that are realizing
that a system built to divide and impoverish and destroy us cannot stand if we do." He thanked "in particular . . . the black women who have spent their lifetimes
dedicated to nurturing everyone before themselves.
We can and will do better for you." He addressed
police misconduct, bravely stating that "police somehow manage to deescalate, disarm, and not kill white
people every day." Williams pledged, "we are going to
have equal rights and justice in our own country or we
will restrict their function and ours." Williams cited
the heinous police killing of 12-year-old Tamir Rice
in Cleveland, saying, "I don't want to hear any more
about how far we've come when paid public servants

can pull a drive-by on a 12-year old playing alone in the park in broad daylight, killing him on television and then going home to make a sandwich." He cited female victims of police brutality, too, like Rekia Boyd and Sandra Bland.

Williams chastised white folk who criticize black social movements like Black Lives Matter, saying that if "you have a critique for the resistance, for our resistance, then you better have an established record of critique of our oppression. If you have no interest in equal rights for black people, then do not make suggestions for those who do. Sit down." Black folk have "been floating this country on credit for centuries, yo, and we're done watching and waiting while this invention called 'whiteness' uses and abuses us, burying black people out of sight and out of mind while extracting our culture, our dollars, our entertainment like oil—black gold, ghettoizing and demeaning our creations then stealing them, gentrifying our genius and then trying us on like costumes before discarding our bodies like rinds of strange fruit." He ended by reminding white America, and millions of black folk, too, that "just because we're magic doesn't mean we're not real."

Williams's activism is homegrown. "That really was kind of just woven into the fabric of my upbringing, my childhood," Williams tells me. "My parents were activists [who] were constantly narrating current events and undergirding those with historical context, and how we got to be where we are, particularly as black people in America. But always viewing ourselves as global citizens, with Africa at the center. But specifically, around liberation movements from Haiti and beyond. So I always had a very significant workload, never from school, always from my parents, that I had to take on at home: reading and writing reports and processing movements throughout history."

Williams talks about going from "the hood in Chicago to moving to a different planet, which was the white suburbs of Massachusetts," saying it "was a discovery mission" about the disparities in treatment between black and white kids—a world he saw up close as a biracial child. "I was able to see all the shit that we would get locked up for and get harassed by cops for and get brought in for and corralled, just for being out in public, laws that were enforced throughout the '80s, certainly, and still to now for black people. And move to the suburbs and seeing how that was encouraged, celebrated and just treated as mischief."

Baldwin was undoubtedly an influence, "one of the most important figures in the history of the world and in my life. But I must admit I came to his actual work later in life than most. I was really raised in many ways by Malcolm and Stokely Carmichael and Fannie Lou Hamer and some other ones." Williams was impressed with how Baldwin negotiated mainstream spaces while managing to bear witness to realities white folk would rather deny. "Between him and Malcolm and my father, certainly, just the forthrightness, of just really just being honest. And there's a difference between truth and meanness. And don't let them convince you that you're being mean just 'cause you walked in the room. That's not an act of aggression. You're allowed to be there."

When Williams accepted his BET Humanitarian Award, he flashed a trait embodied by Belafonte: the willingness to hold fellow artists accountable. Williams chided his fellow entertainers for "dedicating our lives to getting money just to give it right back for someone's brand on our body when we spent centuries praying with brands on our bodies, and now we pray to get paid for brands on our bodies." Belafonte had decades earlier criticized singer Nat King Cole for his "single unfortunate error in judgement."[7] His mistake? Cole had expressed surprise at being attacked onstage by white supremacists when he appeared with a white female singer, arguing, "I can't understand it. Here I have not taken part in any protests. I haven't said anything about civil rights. Nor have I joined an organization fighting segregation. Why should they attack me?"

Belafonte has been on occasion even more forthright in his criticisms of other blacks, especially when he felt they reneged on their duties. In 2002 he caustically accused fellow Jamaican American Colin Powell of abandoning his principles when he served as secretary of state under George Bush. "In the days of slavery, there were those slaves who lived on the plantation and there were those slaves that lived in the house," Belafonte said. "You got the privilege of living in the house if you served the master. Colin Powell's committed to come into the house of the master. When Colin Powell dares to suggest something other than what the master wants to hear, he will be turned back out to pasture."[8] (Powell shot back at Belafonte with characteristic West Indian signifying. A big fan of calypso, Powell maintained that Belafonte's brand was not authentic, and that he preferred the social commentary of the Mighty Sparrow, "the Calypso King.")

Belafonte butted heads more recently with black entertainment royalty when he called out legendary rapper Jay-Z and his superstar entertainer wife, Beyoncé, in 2012 for not being sufficiently active in the movement for change. At a Swiss film festival, after the screening of a documentary about his life, Belafonte was asked at a press conference whether artists today are as committed to social change as those in the '50s and '60s had been. Belafonte said no, and that it was a real shame since there have never been as many black celebrities as today. Belafonte tells me that artists must "give back to the black community, and speak up. Our selfishness is beyond explanation or definition."

Belafonte mentioned Jay-Z and Beyoncé only after being asked about them as representatives of a generation of black artists, but predictably, that response grabbed the most headlines. "Jay-Z took the bait and went public," Belafonte says. "He wrote a song on his very next album where he did everything else but bury me. And [he did] it in a way that tweaked the sensibilities even of his own constituency." Belafonte couldn't have been too surprised by the blowback from Jay-Z when he questioned not only the couple's social responsibility, but their blackness, too, saying, "Give me Bruce Springsteen, and now you're talking. I really think he is black." Jay-Z said that "Bruce Springsteen is a great guy. You're this civil rights activist and you just bigged up the white guy against me in the white media." Belafonte eventually smoothed things over with Jay-Z.

Before Belafonte's challenge, Jay-Z and Beyoncé worked largely behind the scenes to sow good deeds and wield their social influence. But Beyoncé also made a huge splash with a Black Panthers–themed halftime show at Super Bowl 50 that, in homage to Black Lives Matter, vibrated with black political and cultural signifying, just as the video for her song "Formation" dripped with racial meaning by panning to a snatch of graffiti that reads: "Stop shooting us."

When she got blowback for her embrace of BLM politics and her criticism of police misconduct, Beyoncé responded that "I have so much admiration and respect for officers and the families of officers who sacrifice themselves to keep us safe." But then she emphasized her political commitment. "But let's be clear: I am against police brutality and injustice. Those are two separate things. If celebrating my roots and culture during Black History Month made anyone uncomfortable, those feelings were there long before a video and long before me. I'm proud of what we created and I'm proud to be a part of a conversation that is pushing things forward in a positive way."[9]

Jay-Z, too, has been active, spending tens of thousands of dollars to bail out dozens of protesters in Baltimore during Black Lives Matter protests, just as he had done before in Ferguson. In 2008, after three New York cops were acquitted in the death of unarmed citizen Sean Bell, who was shot 50 times on the morning before his wedding, Jay-Z established a trust fund for Bell's two children. Jay-Z's Shawn Carter Foundation provides millions of dollars in scholarships for disadvantaged youth and communities. And both Jay-Z and Beyoncé lent their presence to rallies for Trayvon Martin in the aftermath of his brutal death at the hands of George Zimmerman.

In a manner, Belafonte and Jay-Z are cut from the same cloth. Both were born poor in New York City.

Both are high school dropouts. Both forged careers after finding themselves with vastly different options to social mobility: for Belafonte, a stint in the navy that exposed him to educated black folk speaking about social and racial justice; for Jay, hustling on a street corner selling drugs, where he was exposed to the crudest logic of predatory capitalism. The critical difference is that Belafonte came to maturity in an era when he was radicalized by black thinkers and artists who were part of a stable community that drew from well-established precedents of social change and had the mechanisms in place to achieve political and social transformation. There was a vibrant culture of resistance; there was a vital social movement, including folk like A. Philip Randolph, W.E.B. Du Bois, and especially Paul Robeson, who, in turn, mentored Belafonte. In the aftermath of segregation, those networks were shredded, as huge class chasms emerged in black America, increasingly separating the have-gots from the have-nots. As well-to-do black folk migrated to suburbia from all-black enclaves, working-class and poor black folk were left to fend for themselves without support systems that had been curtailed or jettisoned in the wake of black mobility. These support systems included sororities and fraternities and other voluntary organizations, and informal networks of information and assistance with employment and schooling. With black flight and brain drain from the hood, it was far less likely that a Jay-Z would be mentored by a Harry Belafonte than it was in an earlier day when a Belafonte could be taken under the wing of a Robeson or a Du Bois.

Jay-Z was largely mentored by peers on the streets who inculcated in him the habits, virtues, and dispositions of an urban culture that thrived on cutthroat competition in both underground commerce and informal artistic networks. He was exposed to the allure of financial benefit and material advantage in the hustling lifestyles of New York in the late '80s, just as Ronald Reagan was cementing his agonistic junta through American politics, leaving the poor more destitute and desperate than ever. If Belafonte's salvation lay in connecting with folk who could aid him in his artistic self-realization, Jay-Z's redemption lay in becoming a socially conscientious artist who defends the vulnerable and in parlaying his small fortune into an enterprise, a brand, and, eventually, an empire that continues to astonish with its diversity—from fashion, to a sports agency to luxury alcohol to a music-streaming service.

But all of that offers Jay-Z a perch from which to make influential pronouncements about a criminal justice system that savages black life; it allows him to make records about the heartless denial of opportunity to poor black folk in an American society drunk on its careless righteousness and doomed by its feeble moral vision. The capitulation to capitalism may seem a fait accompli when he asks on his album *4:44*, "What's better than one billionaire?" and then answers, "Two." Jay-Z addresses the racial possibility of generational wealth, and the effort to establish a tradition of inheritance that doesn't depend on political fads or social trends. Such efforts achieve in the boardroom what was fought for in the streets, that is, the economic freedom that civil rights imagined. This is summed up when Jay-Z states, immediately afterward: "'Specially if they're from the same hue as you."

In another manner, Belafonte and Jay-Z are at odds because hip hop is at odds with older forms of cultural expression and racial politics. Black identity took a new turn when hip hop burst onto the national scene. Hip hop culture ripped up the unspoken social agreement that was in place long before the modern civil rights movement. This agreement held that respectability politics was crucial for black success. In the realm of art, that meant that black music and style must cross over, and, at times, defer to, dominant American culture. This agreement insisted that ugly habits and weaknesses—which all groups have, but which were often unfairly used against black folk to prove our pathology—must be shielded from public view. Hip hop insisted on making the family business public and telling the truth about personal weakness and failure while acknowledging big conflicts—of class, of sexuality, of gender, of generation—in black America.

Black folk have never had a single approach to resisting racism, or to explaining, defending, or supporting blackness in private or in public. When hip hop arrived, laced with obscenities, sexual explicitness, abhorrent misogyny, and rage against white racism, it broke with how these matters had often been handled in both bourgeois black culture and among black working-class folk. Our private, internal agonies, ethical anxieties, racial insecurities, and ugly contradictions came roaring out of the black box of respectability. For instance, the color obsession that hounds black circles—an obsession that prizes lighter-skinned folk over darker ones, mixed-race women over black ones, an obsession that betrays surrender to standards of beauty beaten into our brains by the white world—has been relentlessly exposed in the lyrics and visual imagination of hip hop, supposedly the "blackest" art form around.

Ironically, it is the misogyny and materialism of hip hop that reinforces the oppression of women and the undercutting of the poor—thus relieving white folk of the need to perform justice. Paradoxically, artists whose purpose is to bear witness to the tough truth of black life end up purveying its erosion and deterioration; they have a hand in its tainting influence with the spread of animus for black women, half the population of black folk. The white folk who listen may simply follow suit. They don't have to do anything about the status quo they observe in hip hop, a status quo defined by bitterness and hostility for the wombs that gave hip hop artists life.

Hip hop's cultural ubiquity means that black folk are finally no longer invisible; it is surpassing sad that as our presence is embraced in the mainstream we leave unaddressed the very charge of outlaw sexuality for which our black ancestors were hung. The acceptance of outlaw black sexual desire is made into a fetish. For every "bitch" uttered by the artist 21 Savage, for every epithet hurled at women by the rap group Migos, there is complicity in the oppression. Little of what they offer counteracts the corrosive indifference to women's lives. And little of what they say addresses the reasons for the sexual jealousy that caused black harm in a not-too-distant past. Thus, the black body may be sung, may be rapped, may be the object of white desire and material support, but it is not the subject of moral or political redemption. We know this because black bodies killed by the police continue to pile up. Our motives are viewed suspiciously in the broader culture and our humanity is severely doubted. There is, too, in the white view of hip hop, vicarious access to the wildest forms of blackness, and a reverse minstrelsy of sorts: white folk wearing and performing blackness with all of its benefits and none of its burdens. This is what certain forms of the music and culture give rise to, what they authorize in the name of black authenticity. Although they may not have as great a commercial impact as bestselling rappers, there are artists who thrive and are progressive in matters of race and gender, from Common to Talib Kweli and Joey Bada$$, and from Rapsody to Jean Grae and Black Thought.

It would be a mistake to compress the algorithm of Jay-Z's complicated black identity into a broadside against the seductions of capital or to suggest that his blackness is less authentic, less valuable, than Belafonte's blackness. Jay-Z's rise represents the inverted logic of capital finding its agency in the voice and body of a man who comes from a people who were once commodities to be bought and sold; his rise has exposed the central motif of American ambition as hustling. Jay-Z gave a black face to a centuries-old desire—to be on the make, to hustle.[10] Jay-Z forces America to square its conscience with its habits, its forms with its desire. If the American desire for freedom encourages the experiment with as many identities and alternatives as possible, then Jay-Z, far from undercutting the American ideal, is its black apotheosis.

The battle between Belafonte and Jay-Z rests on an unforgiving generational divide. The civil rights generation worked hard to make certain that black images would be protected from the sort of damage it sees hip hop heartily embracing and willfully imposing. Belafonte labored for decades to fight the scourge of white supremacist thinking, to defeat its triumph over a vulnerable black psyche that might be tempted to dance to its own destruction. From the start there was a bitter dispute between black folk who felt that black art should uplift and inspire and those who defended hip hop's right to narrate the dark underside of the American dream and speak from the lingering shadows of poor black existence. The civil rights generation effectively managed a myth of cultural cohesion and group unity in the '60s to generate racial consensus in the battle against white supremacy. But black folk were as divided then as they are now; racial unity has been elusive and fictional, and, arguably, unnecessary to achieve our goals; and the supposed decline of our contemporary era is a golden thread of moral reproof. The times are always in crisis; the youth are forever in rebellion against their elders; the moral atmosphere is always polluted with base and vile visions of life and personal change; and the future is foreboding unless we harken back to standards and ideals we have long since forsaken. It is the role of artists to both puncture this mythology and to weave its most useful strands into a tapestry of moral warning that proves useful for the renewal of struggle against apathy and a reinvigorated enemy.

The real tension between the civil rights generation and the various hip hop generations might have
to do as well with the conflict between stereotypes,
the narrow views of black identity from outside the
culture that must be identified and resisted; archetypes, or virtuous features of black existence defined
from within that should be embraced; and antitypes,
which are often irreverent elements of blackness that
are excluded in the archetypes that respectable black
folk generate. Belafonte fought stereotypes by putting forth valiant and virtuous views of black life and
culture. Jay-Z often appealed to antitypes, irreverent
views of black identity that challenged the respectable images produced in archetypical blackness. Poor
young blacks, and the art that sprang from their quarters, like hip hop, were often left out of archetypical
blackness altogether, or, instead, read as problematic.
It is true that antitypical artists easily adopted troubling aspects of black identity that seem too much
like stereotypes to those who advocate respectability
politics.

It has been intriguing to watch hip hop artists
go from the margins of America to its center. The
same black groups that not a generation ago frowned
on hip hop and dragged hip hop artists before Senate committees to testify about their pathology now
invite them to their conventions and conferences,
toast them at the White House, or welcome them into

boardrooms and elite circles. No single figure is more emblematic of that shift than Jay-Z. A one-time drug dealer who sold crack to children has now cracked the code of respectability to offer children a model of hustling made lyrical, even magical, as he boasts of having the first black president of the United States on speed dial and a corporate black culture at his behest. This is more than the black artist as Horatio Alger, as a rags-to-riches story updated for the hood. It is also about the black artist as the fleshly intersection of splendidly complicated visions of blackness that can never be dismissed or underestimated, pigeonholed or predicted.

Jay-Z's prominence hinges on far more than his brash embrace of capitalism; it rides, too, on the way he has managed to do what not even Harry Belafonte did: tell the truth about black folk in the art itself. Belafonte brilliantly experimented with various forms of musical expression, from mento to calypso, from blues to jazz, from swing to bebop, and his use of pop art forms to articulate his vision of blackness was exhilarating and astonishingly vital. His command of the work songs and spirituals, of the ballads and folktales of the people in forging his art, is edifying. Still, Belafonte could barely make a frontal assault, lyrically speaking, on the domain of white supremacy. He fought it by inference and implication, by signifying gestures and romantic alliances that undercut the mythology of purity that traced around white words, ideas, and bodies. He did it early on by embracing the bebop that was both a stylistic rebellion against swing and a racial complaint about the music's appropriation by white artists. The jutting rhythms and crosscutting cadences, the dramatic shifts in speed and intensity, the laconic swoops and knifing, jarring paces made jazz a blacker music once again.

Belafonte had to consistently camouflage his radical politics to avoid being found out as a progressive. In his youth, he and his family had to exploit their ambiguous racial identity in order to live in white neighborhoods that didn't rent to black folk, and to gain admission to white schools that didn't admit Negroes, donning a racial and political masquerade that was critical at points to his personal and artistic survival.

What Belafonte did with style and signification Jay-Z has managed to do with substance and lyric. While Jay-Z is best known for his insistence on the centrality of hustling—he was never anything but a "nigger," and, more usefully, a "nigga"; for him, the camouflage was a hustling aesthetic that eventually made clear that the entire nation was a hustle, and thus, Jay-Z was ahead of the game. Lacking the credentials to pass ethnically like Belafonte, he delved far more deeply into his degraded status as America's nigger. If Baldwin claimed that America fabricated the nigger to justify the exploitation of black folk, then

Jay-Z, or more exactly, the younger Shawn Carter, is the scary imagination of white America come alive; he is the specter in the flesh of the profane, obscene, immoral, and illegal creature that so many white folk feared. There is nothing hidden about Jay-Z; he is the explicit repudiation of every strategy of respectability politics and racial and artistic camouflage. He told the truth about black suffering and aspiration in his lyrics. He expressed the ideals and desires of the black poor.

But from the beginning, Jay-Z also mixed in political messages with his hustling agenda. On a freestyle over Lil Wayne's "A Milli" beat, Jay acknowledges that he could suffer the same fate as Sean Bell, linking commerce, crime, cops, and Obama's presidency. "Shawn Carter, Sean Bell/What's the difference? Do tell," he raps. "50 shots or 50 mill; ain't no difference go to hell." On "Watch Me," Jay laments that "they gon' kill us anyway," and that "Them cops uptown hit homes with forty-one rounds," speaking of African immigrant Amadou Diallo, who was shot 41 times. On "Minority Report," Jay wonders what might have happened had President Bush's plane run out of fuel when he was flying over New Orleans after Hurricane Katrina, suggesting that "He'd be just another Bush surrounded by a couple orchids." He joined Bono and Rihanna on "Stranded (Haiti Mon Amour)" and greeted them with the familiar saying, "Sak pasé, my Port-Au-Princess," offering condolences "as you fightin' against this." On "Ballad for a Fallen Solider," Jay claimed that "Bin Laden been happenin' in Manhattan," suggesting a parallel between political terror and the terror in the streets, arguing that "Crack was anthrax back then," referring to the time when the police "was Al Qaeda to black men."

If Belafonte conceived his duty to represent black interests and images with dignity and grace, then Jay-Z's ethic of representation consists of bearing witness to the despised denizen of the hood. If Belafonte's "black modern urbanity" tapped into earlier forms of bebop and blues music and black creations, then Jay-Z's black postmodern urbanism reflects the will to combat white supremacy, on record, by name, in ways that Belafonte's generation hardly did. Jay-Z and his generation articulate direct messages of racial resistance and black assault upon the bigoted premises and racist conclusions of art, life, and culture. In a sense, it was not Belafonte but Lorraine Hansberry who, in a direct address to Bobby Kennedy, prefigured the bold gestures of defiant blackness that sprang up in hip hop.

Hansberry ended the meeting between Kennedy and the Negro collective with a majestic flourish. After Jerome Smith testified to the horrific treatment *of black males* by white bigots, his valiant monologue had hushed most everyone in the room. On the heels of his witness, Hansberry poignantly foreshadowed how we grapple in our day with the slippery intersections of gender, race, class, and sexual orientation.

"That is all true," Hansberry acknowledged Smith's words as she rose, "but I am not worried about black men—who have done splendidly, it seems to me, all things considered."

Hansberry broke faith with the conspiracy of masculine pronouns to exhaust all human experience. She took a stand to liberate grammar from its disrespect of female users. Flashing her theater chops, Hansberry paused for dramatic effect. She looked at Bobby Kennedy, who, for the first time that night, looked at her.

"But I am very worried about the state of the civilization which produced that photograph of the white cop standing on that Negro woman's neck in Birmingham."

Then she smiled and extended her hand.

"Goodbye, Mr. Attorney General," she offered, and turned and walked out.

"We followed her," Baldwin says.

One can imagine the shiver sent through the room.

Hansberry snapped them from an unthinking identification of the state of black men with the state of the race. With a single sentence, she commanded us to picture black women's bodies as the home of zigzagging cultural crosscurrents and the fierce interweaving of region, gender, morality, race, policing, violence, image, anxiety, and civilization. The artist in Hansberry saw in the photograph of a black woman being manhandled by white cops all the suffering, all the injustice, all the offense to black life. The brutality was grave enough; the spread of the image transmitted trauma and reinforced the vulnerability of black women and, indeed, the race.

Neither Hansberry nor Baldwin were done with commenting on the power of the visual. Not long afterward, both Hansberry and Baldwin got involved in projects involving images and race: Baldwin teamed with his high school classmate Richard Avedon to produce an intimate visual exploration of social change in the bodies of black and white folk in America, with a deeply probing, highly emotional, freewheeling essay by Baldwin. Hansberry, too, would collaborate with a slew of photographers in the book *The Movement,* sponsored by SNCC and penned while she was dying from cancer.[11] The urgency of the harrowing afternoon Baldwin and Hansberry spent together in the Kennedy apartment bled into their prose and shaped their interpretations.

Hansberry captured in her remark a transcendent wisdom that instructs us today. If the transition between the civil rights and hip hop generations has to do, in part, with how the black artist is conceived as a representative figure, then the complications of black identity mean that such representation can never be easy or simple. The way black representation had been colored by male experience reinforced the belief that blackness speaks only, or at best, in a baritone voice. All of this muted the interests and intelligence of more than half the race. Maleness has functioned in our race much like whiteness has in the larger culture: its privileges have been rendered normal, its perspectives natural, its biases neutral, its ideas superior, its anger wholly justifiable, and its way of being the gift of God to the universe. Hansberry shattered that compact, not so much in her art onstage, which she didn't live long enough to fully explore, but in essays that touched on feminism and identity, and in the allusiveness of her comment that day. If our male experience is taken for granted by us as the lens and length of our people's experience, it has been seen by others that way too. Bobby Kennedy was in agreement with Baldwin and most of his mates that what happened to the black race is what happened to black men, and that women and children were satellites that orbited around the universe of masculine priorities and perceptions.

When Lyndon Johnson aide Daniel Moynihan issued his famous report on the black family a couple of years later, his warning that a quickly developing matriarchy would rattle the black family presumed the legitimacy of measuring the health of black life through society's impact on its males. Hansberry's significant sentence was a prebuttal to Moynihan's report; it was an opening salvo of a feminism that gave weight to black female experience at a time when black men and white men, and often white women, too, agreed about the relative value of black women and girls. That compact has held to this day, splintered only when the voices of black women interrupt the "natural" course of things in our communities, when women have risen to say *no more, not this*—have rejected a state of affairs where women and girls are secondary. Hansberry's words were her version of #MeToo.

It has been extremely difficult for black folk to follow Hansberry's lead in insisting that women and girls matter. Neither Belafonte's generational edicts of representation, nor Jay-Z's, have grappled with how gender figures into the role of the black artist. When gender is at play, which is to say, always, we do a poor job of discerning the big and small offenses that knock women and girls off-kilter, that make their lives even more tedious than race has already made them, that wear them down to accept the preference for men's ways and the unquestioned fulfillment of men's desires.

As hip hop has made clear—and black religion, too, for that matter—when we conceive of the horrors we confront, they have a masculine tint; we measure the terrors we face by calculating their harm to our men and boys. Thus the role of our artists has often been limited to validating the experiences, expressions, and desires of boys and men. When we name those plagued by police violence, we cite the names of the boys and men but not the names of the girls and women. We take special note of how black boys are unfairly kicked out of school while ignoring that our girls are right next to them in the line of expulsion. We empathize with black men who end up in jail because of a joint they smoked while overlooking the defense against domestic abuse that lands just as many women in jail. We offer authority and celebration to men at church to compensate for how the white world overlooks their talents unless they carry a ball or a tune. We thank black fathers for lovingly parenting their children, and many more of them do so than is recognized in the broader world, which is one reason for our gratitude. But we are relatively thankless for the near superhuman efforts of our mothers to nurture and protect us.

Baldwin was a black homosexual male in public at a time when there was little precedent for any major figure being openly gay, much less the most celebrated black writer in the land. Baldwin's gay identity caused quite a bit of blowback from black male leaders and writers. The NAACP's Roy Wilkins didn't like Baldwin because he was gay; the writer was disparaged as "Martin Luther Queen" in the civil rights world.[12] Ralph Ellison declared in a 1953 letter to fellow writer Albert Murray that Baldwin "doesn't know the difference between getting religion and going homo."[13]

Hansberry was a lesbian, privately negotiating her queer identity while married to the Jewish writer Robert Nemiroff.[14] There was even less space for her to reckon with her sexual desires in the confines of a culture that extracted a pound of flesh for each layer of her three-tiered oppression: black, female, lesbian. Hansberry secretly penned letters in 1957 to *The Ladder,* the first subscription-based lesbian publication in the nation, charting the intricate interrelationship between color, gender, and sexual orientation. She identified with the feminist movement taking root in the late 1950s, arguing that "the most oppressed group of any oppressed group will be its women," saying that the "twice oppressed" often become "twice militant."[15] Or, in her case, triply so.

Queer blackness is still problematic, still a threat, in America. It is often our queer writers and artists who compel us to take note of our hypocrisy and bigotry, whether it is Janet Mock bearing witness to the tribulations and triumphs of being a black trans person, or writers Alice Walker and Jacqueline Woodson embodying the elegant righteousness of their lesbian identity and politics. Blackness and queerness have been intimate for far longer than the formal recognition that either identity has existed. None of the philosophical briefs against sexual difference rooted in nationalist or pan-African identity can possibly destroy the evidence of its opposite: countless unions within the same sex, intimacies between partners otherwise described as mere friends, homoerotic signifying within heterosexual contexts.

In many ways, queer blackness is the perfect metaphor for blackness writ large—a blackness that was from the start seen as strange, exotic, dangerous, challenging, and subversive. Given the ravages of hip hop—its persistent misogyny and rampant homophobia—the genre does not offer the ideal forum to express the complex identities of black folk.

But there is a strong ray of hope in hip hop's adaptation to venues other than the concert stage or the recording booth.

Few, if any, cultural productions have garnered as much press or praise over the last decade as the Broadway musical *Hamilton,* based on the colorful life of Founding Father Alexander Hamilton. Lin-Manuel Miranda, a genius with outsize gifts for writing, composing, singing, acting, and rapping, reimagined Hamilton's life as an archetypal hip hop narrative of rags to riches that was more Biggie Smalls than Horatio Alger. *Hamilton* seized the nation's imagination precisely because Miranda retrofitted the American dream with a hip hop vocabulary, cadence, and flow. The very people who were denied access to the nation's bounty and social legitimacy gained their rhetorical revenge through Miranda, son of a politician who came to New York from Puerto Rico, casting the American dream as the black, brown, and immigrant's story.

"Hip hop, for those who are practitioners or who grew up just living in it, has always been, at least for me in my experience, a way of sorting out thoughts," Daveed Diggs says to me. He originally portrayed Marquis de Lafayette/Thomas Jefferson in *Hamilton*.

> I used to teach rap classes to middle-schoolers all the time. And the crazy thing that you would see with kids that age is they're at the stage where nobody really cares what they have to say, but they can totally make the same kind of judgments and form opinions about everything happening in society that everybody else can. So you frame it in this way that is virtuosic because hip hop is really about virtuosity. And that's one of the things that *Hamilton* did as well, and that I think Lin is arguing is also the basis for the founding of this country. Because it was done through language. It was about people writing back and forth to each other. And people who could share their ideas

in the most impressive way were the people
that won it.

The cast of those who won looked dramatically different in *Hamilton,* permitting Miranda to use his racial and musical imagination to reconceive the color and cadence of democracy.

> I think putting black and brown and non-white
> bodies on these characters of the founding fa-
> thers, and then having them present the same
> ideas that they were presenting at the time and
> to speak in today's version of virtuosity, was
> part of the political discussion that *Hamilton*
> allowed in some spaces where it hadn't hap-
> pened yet. And it gave ownership over those
> ideas to a lot of us who didn't feel any sense
> of ownership over it—myself included. It was
> of great use for me to have to perform them
> in that way. I feel more American myself and I
> think it possibly had that effect on a lot of other
> people.

Leslie Odom, Jr., who portrayed Aaron Burr in the original production, agrees with Diggs that hip hop is a language that articulates perfectly American ideals, and forces us to see what's truly American about kids who've been outlawed because of their skin.

"What we need so desperately is to recast the vision of, to reimagine the possibilities for these young brothers and these young sisters that we see on the street corner, on the school bus, on the subway," Odom tells me. "Lin is messing with whatever your image might be of what's possible for these rappers, for these black and brown people who like this kind of music, that speak in this way. He's sort of, rightfully so, putting the label of revolutionary, of leader, on Kendrick and Kanye and Jay-Z and Biggie and Tupac and Nas. He's reminding us that these people do more than just make music that entertains us. They speak for a group of people."

Renee Elise Goldsberry thinks that art plays a huge role in changing our lives too.

"If we can see ourselves in our history, then there's some hope of learning, right?" Goldsberry, who originally played Angelica Schuyler, tells me.

> And so if those guys are played by us, and we see that they were rebels! All we know of them as is the winners. The slave owners. They're the man now. So what can we learn from them, how can we see ourselves in them? But in that moment in history, that's not who they were. They were the voice of protest. They were the "kill me, I'll die for this." They were the ones whose pants were, you know, hanging down.

And we don't see them as that until we actually embody them. It's a beautiful thing to see
America [this way].

"There was a Baldwin quote I actually retweeted
this morning that speaks to exactly what you're talking about," Lin-Manuel Miranda tells me the day we
talk.

The quote is: "Whatever you describe to another person is also a revelation of who you
are and who you think you are. You cannot
describe anything without betraying your
point of view, your aspirations, your fears,
yours hopes, everything." I follow and I just
love that quote. Because that's how I saw Hamilton. I didn't know anything about that dude
except he was the guy on the ten. I knew he
had died in a duel. I wrote a paper on him in
eleventh grade. I knew his son died in a duel,
then he died in a duel. And that was enough
to get [Ron Chernow's] *Alexander Hamilton*
off the shelf and into my hands . . . How do
you lose your son to this and then die of the
same thing? What leads to that mistake? And
then when I opened the book and realized this
dude was born in the Caribbean, this guy has
a tragic childhood that rivals anything from

Dickens and anything from our hip hop heroes who have overcome struggle. Whether
it's Marcy or Eight Mile or Queensbridge or,
for Scarface, the South. And then when I got
to the part where he writes about a hurricane,
and everyone takes up a collection to get him
out, I started tearing up and I felt, "That's the
most hip hop shit I ever heard." This is a guy
who writes about his struggle so specifically
and well that he transcends. And that's what
our favorite rappers do. They're writers who
write about the struggle so well that they tran-
scend the struggle. And they make the specific
universal. So a kid who grows up in the suburb
of Long Island, listens to "Juicy," and understands what it feels like.

Chernow's book inspired Miranda to rethink the
cultural and racial contexts of American identity.

I had that epiphany at the end of the second
chapter of Chernow's book. And then it just
kept proving me right. Oh, and then he writes
essays about the Revolution. Oh, and then he
gets the attention of Washington. And then he
defends the Constitution. He writes the Fed-
eralist papers. I mean, he writes with other
people, but he writes most of it. And I was like,

"This is a motherfuckin' writer." And he can't stop. And he also writes his way into trouble. It's that other part of hip hop too—like battling. And so as soon as he wrote his way off the island I thought, one, this reminds me of my favorite MCs and two, it reminds me of my father. Because my father got a full ride to NYU when he was seventeen years old in Puerto Rico. Because there was a scout looking to increase diversity at NYU and saw my dad. And basically he got a full education here in New York but he didn't speak a word of English. He learned English while he was getting his grad degree. People think I'm busy, or like I work hard. I'm the fucking slacker of my family when compared to my father's story and my mother's story. So I think back to that Baldwin quote of, everything you write betrays how you feel. The thing that keeps popping up in my work is this awe for the immigrant experience. This awe for people who can start from scratch, in a land where maybe they don't know the language, and create a life, and actually shape the world they moved to. And to me Hamilton is like the extreme proto-immigrant story.

If the Broadway musical proved a powerful artistic outlet to engage race and ethnicity, the Hollywood blockbuster proved to be an unexpected ally in the representation of edifying and complicated blackness. *Black Panther* is a film that is so much more than a movie—it is a seismic cultural moment, an artistic document that captures the Black Zeitgeist. I ask the film's star, Chadwick Boseman, about the literally world-altering nature of the fame that has made him the hottest star on the globe right now—the hunger among black people for the affirmation the film brings is unprecedented—and he is characteristically humble. But he saw in the film the chance to delve deeply into the myriad dimensions of black life precisely because the African nation of Wakanda is fictional.

"Because it's fantasy, there's an opportunity for you to pull from everything that you know from your African Studies, everything you know about the culture, and you can grow inside the creative process." The tragedy, of course, is that not too many know their African Studies, since the motherland remains— for too many folk, even, we must admit, for many of our own people—the dark continent. It was ignorance about black life that plagued the meeting with Kennedy too. But *Black Panther*'s fictional setting not only sets our imaginations free, it reinforces the idea that race is a fiction, that color is, as Baldwin insisted, a political identity projected from the imagination, too, not from wombs and chromosomes and the like. As much as black folk have eagerly embraced *Black Panther* for the freedom it grants us to hunger out loud for the mother milk of black-on-black love, the kind of love that Baldwin, and Hansberry, and Belafonte, and so many others unashamedly and unapologetically reveled in, Boseman believes that we can embrace our freedom of self-expression whenever we want without the white world's permission. It is, after all, the premise of *Black Panther,* and, it seems, the bedrock of Boseman's aesthetic vision.

"If I'm a painter, I don't need permission to paint. I can get a canvas—I can use a wall—and I can create something, and I can explore myself, my identity, whatever that expression is, without permission. I can do the same thing as a writer. Very often when you talk to actors, they forget that they don't need permission." An artist need only have herself and another person, and if, in Greek theater, for instance, there's a chorus, that's even better. Boseman acknowledges that commerce impinges on the artistic process, and that while his ideal of creative expression works best in smaller venues with lower budgets, the canvas for *Black Panther* is much larger. It doesn't just have a much bigger budget, but its canvas is the collective imagination of a black diaspora that spans the globe. "The fact that this is being done on this level with this amount of money behind it, resources behind it, marketing behind it—that's what makes this a unique experience."

But there's another sort of permission that *Black Panther* refuses to ask—the permission to walk down suburban streets where black bodies seem out of place, to inhabit black neighborhoods where the addition of black homes is neither gentrification nor integration but the status quo, to live and breathe and love and think and fight our way to our most fulfilling destinies. And, most uplifting, there is no necessary reference to whiteness. Wakanda is a black world that takes blackness as the norm.

> I think what's unique about this particular achievement with *Black Panther* is that it's aspirational in a way where it doesn't ask anybody for permission. Wakanda exists without Europe, without white people. Wakanda doesn't exist because they were trying to protect themselves from the outside world of colonization and slavery. Their protection was because of vibranium [a fictional metal from which Black Panther's suit is made]. It just so happens that in protecting this resource, they also protected themselves from those things that have been a Maafa [African Holocaust of enslavement] for us, that have taken us through colonization, through the Middle Passage, through slavery. So Wakanda exists without the white man as

a context. That's part of what's revolutionary
about it: there is a Wakanda "even if."

The fact that *Black Panther* had a $200 million bud-
get not only makes it the most expensive film ever directed by a black director, but it confirms that when
cash matches consciousness the combination has the
potential to shred stereotypes—just as Belafonte and
Hansberry attempted to do—and to present a far more
sophisticated vision of blackness. *Black Panther* offers
a vision of blackness that is at once Afro-futuristic,
since it projects black folk in the science and technology of the future; Afro-gnostic, since it presents
a universe teeming with the inspiration to gain black
knowledge, which is really human knowledge; Afro-
pessimistic, since blackness is a resilient and flexible
identity and not merely a static object of admiration or
exploitation; Afro-realistic, since blackness is the cumulative consequence of all done to, and through, and
because of it; and Afro-idealistic, because blackness
supplies the norms and goals of the culture when we
pursue our self-expression as far as our imaginations
can take us.

Just as Belafonte had to wrestle with which roles
to play, and which to leave aside, Boseman faces that
choice even today, some 50 years later. He recounts
being offered a role in a two-person film with a huge
white star. The producer swore that it would be great

for his career, and that his role was just as good as the white actor's part. When he received the script, he discovered that his character couldn't read, couldn't drive, and, inexplicably, couldn't swim, and yet he was supposed to be a street-savvy mover and shaker who was knowledgeable about money. Since the pitch was that the film couldn't get made without him, he took delight in being the person to stop it from seeing the cinematic light of day.

He also takes delight in seeing black folk make a festival of their *Black Panther* theater experience. Some fans are dressing in traditional African garb as the film offers them entrée into the communal wear and social bonding usually fostered by rites of passage ceremonies.

> Film is an extension of theater. Theater is an extension of ritual. Ritual is an extension of culture. As black people we're talking back to the screen as if it's a theater and you're going to get that immediate response. But [black folk attending showings of *Black Panther*] has become a carnival, in the best sense of the word.

If carnival captures the vibrancy of black culture, satire, too, permits the black artist to offer a complicated take on black identity and culture. *Key & Peele* is a television sketch comedy show that ran for five seasons and provided a forum for two brilliant artists, Keegan-Michael Key and Jordan Peele, to explore race and American identity. "In so many generations and for much of human history, one form of satire is that old adage: a spoonful of sugar makes the medicine go down," Key tells me. "You would never laugh at something that doesn't resonate with you in a positive or negative way. And I think that humor, especially in the form of satire—as opposed to parody—has been helpful for people of all different walks of life, whether they're a person of color or a person who's downtrodden, a person who's poor."

Key believes that humor can provoke serious reflection on our culture. "I don't know when this future comes, but I see the future that RFK could not realize, because his life was cut so short. And that James Baldwin could not realize 'cause his life was cut short. It's a future that we're hurtling toward. And the reason we're in the fraught political and social time that we're in right now is because the old guard is dying. And the old guard is not in a position to regain power. It's trying. I'm a full believer that what we're experiencing now are the last gasps. And so humor's job is to reflect what society is, in all of its facets, in the present."

Key argues that humor has a clarifying effect, too, making us see that issues we often mistake for race are really class issues. "I feel it's a misnomer to say lots of things are race issues, when they're class issues.

Don't nobody get that wrong, there are race issues! I'm looking for the news where a bunch of white dudes that run away from cops get shot in the back. Now, they commit more crimes. We don't hear about that either. But part and parcel of them committing those crimes is that they're poor. And so there shouldn't be a difference between a poor black man and a poor white man. The difference is, when that poor white man robs a store and runs, ain't no one shooting him in the back. That's racism." But it is the cultural angle that offers the comic a way into an issue that can yield the greatest laughter and, thus, the greatest possibility of grappling with a particular issue. "It's my job to look at the cultural facets as deeply as I can. So that I can draw a comparison between a person of color and a person who's Caucasian. Or [between] a person who's Hispanic and a person who's Caucasian. Because, really, what do I want to do? I want to make the most amount of people laugh. And the way to do that is culturally."

Key thinks that there is a paradox to representing blackness in humor: one aims for universal laughter and the racial element takes care of itself. It seems to harken back to the early days of Bill Cosby, when he decided not to use race as a crutch in his humor and instead sought a universal register. "In *Key & Peele* we collectively never said, 'It's not black enough yet.' We only ever said it's not funny enough yet. If you make the premise clever enough and undeniable enough, then you can put black folk in the sketch and it'll appeal to everyone. I've met brothers who've said to us, 'I don't understand how you two brothers did this. How did you make it mainstream first and then cross over to black people?' And the answer to the question is, 'Because funny's funny.'"

Key & Peele also used art to tackle taboo subjects. In one sketch, *Key & Peele* tackle the thorny subject of the slave auction of black bodies where the enslaved wonder why they're not being chosen. "It's really subverting that idea [of enslavement]. Because it plumbs a more human emotion than just the predicament the men found themselves in."

Key even sees the universal dimensions of the most racially resonant and highly charged role he played: Luther, President Barack Obama's fictional anger translator who channeled the first black president's masked beliefs and hidden emotions.

"Wouldn't the junior mechanic in Sparksburg, Louisiana, who has to listen to his boss, who's a dummy, want an anger translator too? . . . That's the appeal of Luther. It happens to be in an African American construct, but the universal construct on top of it is this: Wouldn't we all like to have an anger translator?"

The fact that both Key and Peele are biracial offers them a privileged position in observing race and addressing blackness in their art. "I think Jordan coined this phrase once: we're racial referees. Simply because we exist, we sit on the outside of either norm—what the 'black' norm is, or the 'mainstream' norm is. So we've been given passports to both countries."

If Key and Peele are racial referees, then Jordan Peele is the ultimate race game official in his masterly first film, *Get Out,* a powerful guide to the black and white universe. Because it wrestles with race in such a sophisticated and cosmopolitan fashion, *Get Out* has become a language of racial demystification and signifying, a way to decode the esoteric meanings of blackness and to decipher the arcane horrors of whiteness. "I start with the understanding, or the premise, that conversation, art, expression is the most powerful weapon we have against violence and oppression," Peele tells me. "That our words, whether it's words on a page, or words spoken, or words from a color in a paintbrush, are just more powerful. That's what I learned from Martin Luther King, Jr. That's what I learned from the Bible."

Get Out is the perfect horror film since it teems with the tropes of enslavement and the auction block, when black bodies were snatched into this country, into our terror. That reference to horror movies is deliberate; our existence here has been a string of horror flicks. *Body Snatchers. Night of the Living Dead. The (Slave) Cabin in the Woods. The (Big) House of the Devil. The (White) Others. Dawn of the Dead. You're*

Next. Alien. Nightmare on Elm Street, and at whatever address we have lived. This is why black direc-
tors hardly ever make horror films. They know the
formula. The black character dies first, or certainly
earlier than the white ones, is often alone with no
partner, exists awkwardly in the white world, brings
comic relief, and is only seen as authentic if she speaks
in vernacular. Except that is no horror film; that is the
real-life drama we have lived for the last 400 years.

Peele creates art that registers the violence done to
black identity. "So when I'm writing a comedy sketch
or when I'm writing a movie, I'm trying to basically bite
off a premise, a risky idea or notion. And it's risky because I've never seen it before. So with a sketch it might
be, how do I address police violence against African
Americans? The thing that's not ever going to be funny
in a million years: real horror. But I possess this nag-
ging force in my head that says there's a way to make
anything entertaining. And you can do it without demeaning the victims of these crimes . . . If it hits on
some underlying real shit, no one can have a problem
with that . . . at the very least there will be discussions
that can happen in a world where that movie exists,
that can't happen in a world where that movie has
never existed."

Get Out is a satire on white liberals seen through
the eyes of a black protagonist, Chris, as he visits
his white girlfriend's parents over a weekend and

discovers the horrors that await black folk who dare to naïvely trust well-intentioned white folk. *Get Out* is a tale that draws energy from undoing the post-racial myths of the Obama era and yet speaks perfectly to the Age of Trump, with its fastidious falseness of concern for true democracy, with its truncated vision of blackness, with its hateful impulses unleashed in the collective id of a nation on the brink of moral paralysis. "There was this idea that engaging in racial discussion and calling out racism would be perpetuating the problem. This notion of 'Why do we still have to talk about race? Aren't we done with that? Aren't we over it? We've got this black president.' And it was sufficiently silenced. We had Donald Trump, a public figure, accusing the president of not being from this country. There's a whole faction of people who are being validated in their racist sentiments. And that's what grew to today. We knew if someone broke that silence people would respond to it. Luther said what was on the president's mind, in our opinion, but he said what we all were thinking as well when he was calling out the bigoted haters of Obama."

Get Out brilliantly sets up the black body as the domain of a symbiotic whiteness, a whiteness that seeks the black body to host its deepest desires. The film begins in the suburbs, which has often been a site of utter terror for black bodies, an unsafe zone of symbolic whiteness that purges black presence, steals black futures, and leaves black bodies for dead. "The first scene is a black man walking through the suburbs. And we've all just been dealing with the tragedy of Trayvon. It's such an absurdly horrific incident that it's at home in a horror movie. It's at home in a thriller. And furthermore, to put everybody, whoever you are—black, white—in the shoes of that character, to feel what that feels like, I knew was going to set the rest of the movie off from that context. So after that scene, we'd all be black. Everybody watching the movie is black. White people for the first time are understanding, are fearing for this character in the suburbs."

The skepticism of whiteness abounds in *Get Out*; everywhere there is creeping suspicion and distrust of the liberal enthusiasm for black existence. *Get Out* presents appropriation as more than a symbolic gesture of cultural envy; it is a Freudian feast of psychic distortion and mental occupation, a morphology of racial fibers and nerves, an anthropology of absorption that feasts on the metaphoric and literal insides, and remains, of black life.

The greatest loss, the greatest theft, is the silencing of the black voice in the infamous sunken place. "When I first wrote the concept of the sunken place, I thought a lot about the prison industrial complex. And I thought about the lack of representation of black skin and voices and perspective in film . . . Chris is down there, and when he screamed, it was silent. You couldn't hear his cries. That, to me, became a symbol for taking away our greatest weapon against injustice—our voices. And we've seen it when Colin Kaepernick or other athletes are called 'sons of bitches' for kneeling in peaceful protest. It's textbook 'sunken place.' Why are they scared of expression? When [former ESPN television host] Jemele Hill was put on suspension for saying the president is racist, it's taking away the voice. Because they know that's the most powerful thing."

Get Out is populated with the folklore of white accretions and subtractions, the buildup of white possessions, the most prized being the black bodies white people seek to empty of black souls. The film also portrays the release of white fears of extinction into the bodies of black folk forced to host white culture's pathological urge to unite. This is a reversal of the usual route of race in America: instead of the forced busing of black bodies into white neighborhoods, this is the coerced integration of white minds and black bodies. In the end, it is everyday blackness, mundane and ordinary blackness, that saves the day, as the working man, the often maligned and looked-down-on TSA agent, not the black professional, uses his gifts and instincts to rescue Chris.

Black artists have consistently sought to uplift the redemptive dimensions of black life even as they seek to defend black culture from the vicious assaults from hostile forces. The impact the black artist may make can be glimpsed when Beyoncé presented Colin Kaepernick with the *Sports Illustrated* Muhammad Ali Legacy Award. "It's been said that racism is so American that when we protest racism," Beyoncé said, "some assume we're protesting America."[16] Our artists, like our thinkers and activists, have expended great energy to set things right and clarify the stakes of our struggle and debate.

THE INTELLECTUALS

BLACK ON BLACK MINDS

N one of the other figures James Baldwin called to the meeting possessed the gravitas of Kenneth Clark—the most celebrated social psychologist in the land. Clark's presence seemed to promise a fair hearing of the issues that Kennedy wanted to discuss, many of which Clark would address in his 1965 classic, *Dark Ghetto.* He was seen as a successor to heralded Swedish economist Gunnar Myrdal, author of the classic study *An American Dilemma: The Negro Problem and Modern Democracy,* which argued that America is dedicated to a creed of rights and opportunity for all yet falls short in applying it to the Negro. Clark was a brilliant scholar whose empirical studies of racial inequality in social structures and institutional networks garnered academic prestige. He and his wife, Mamie, pioneered research on the effect of sustained prejudice on black children, fueling the Supreme Court's groundbreaking 1954 *Brown v. Board of Education* decision outlawing segregation in the nation's public schools.

Clark was clear about what a black thinker should do. "The Negro intellectual . . . cannot confuse his role with that of the politician or the mass leader." The Negro intellectual must "interpret, supplement, and give substance to the work of these leaders." In fact, the Negro intellectual "has no choice but to accept the challenge of trying to help America survive. This is his commitment and obligation to himself, to his race, to his nation, and to his world." Clark's definition of the intellectual's role fit nicely with the meeting's purpose from Kennedy's point of view. But Clark did not get much of a chance to speak. All of the points he planned to make about the furious analytical contradictions at the heart of the urban crisis brewing in black America were suffocated by the personal and group witness to the suffering that the masses of black folk silently endured. As the rebellions and uprisings that dotted the social horizon in the sixties would soon prove, that silence wouldn't last long. At their meeting, Baldwin's brand of autobiographical assertion and moral witness—transmuted in searing bursts by Smith and brilliantly adapted by Hansberry—won the day. For Baldwin, intellectuals—by which I mean folk like academics, artists, ministers, prophets, and others who think intently for a living—weren't merely objective analysts at a distance from their object of inquiry, but rather deeply invested thinkers who use reasoned emotion to explain the world.[1]

Neither could one blame maverick political figures for seeking an alternative to black leaders who used the carefully calculated civil rights rhetoric of the day. If Bobby Kennedy wanted to bask in Baldwin's brilliance, he was hardly alone. The nation was taken with the literary firebrand. In a profile published in *Esquire* magazine in August 1964, the month Baldwin turned 40, Marvin Elkoff captured his astonishing ascent to fame:

> No Negro writer or spokesman has had so great an impact on the entire white liberal world as James Baldwin. He is the first who has gotten beneath their skin, or forced them into his, the first to make them see what it is like to be a Negro in America. A *Time* cover, a *Life* spread, TV appearances by the score, invitations by the hundred to drawing rooms and lecture halls—rarely, in fact, has any American writer had so much public renown. And rarely has there been a more unlikely prospect for the honor.[2]

Was it Baldwin's lack of formal education that made him "unlikely" to be honored? Or the fact that he was a queer black figure who wasn't the sort of manly candidate for reverence that his sometime nemesis Norman Mailer strove to be? In any case, there was, predictably, harsh criticism of Baldwin, and often vicious blowback: vitriol, jealousy, contempt. With his recent renaissance, one may think that Baldwin was always as popular as he is now, when, indeed, he had "fallen, in recent years, out of favor and off of syllabi." The times had to catch up to Baldwin; the Black Lives Matter movement has made Baldwin's fusion of political combat and existential witness relevant again.[3]

* * *

When Baldwin sat on a roundtable sponsored by *Commentary* magazine in 1964 to discuss "Liberalism & the Negro" with philosopher Sidney Hook, sociologist Nathan Glazer, and economist Gunnar Myrdal, he worried out loud, "What the hell [am I] supposed to say to them in there about all this sociology and economics jazz?"

The intellectual historian Harold Cruse took the occasion of Baldwin's performance anxiety to slight the writer as a lightweight thinker out of his depth. "This failure to discuss the racial conflicts either in terms of possible practical solutions, or in terms of American economic and sociological realities, made Baldwin's assault on white liberals a futile rhetorical exercise: it was further weakened by the intellectual inconsistencies, incoherence and emotionalism of his line of argument."[4] *Commentary* editor Norman Podhoretz said, "I purposely got Jimmy [Baldwin] to the seminar to get him off that personal kick and make him talk about solutions and programs. It didn't work."[5] There was only one problem with their critiques—they weren't true.

Baldwin met his intellectual confreres blow for blow and exposed their lack of knowledge of black lives and black thought, of what real flesh and blood Negroes believed about race and how that shaped their behavior. Hook, for example, argued that "the case against discrimination rests fundamentally on ethical premises," that such a belief fuels "an equality of concern on the part of the community for each individual within it to develop his capacities to their greatest reach," and that this view of liberalism hardly denied "the notion that Negroes might receive temporary help to improve their condition."[6] Hook compared the Negro plight to that of victims of a natural disaster, or to German immigrants arriving during and after World War II who were offered jobs that others in the community were just as qualified to fill. Hook drew the line at permanent preferential treatment for Negroes. He said it disrespected Negroes to lower standards for them in the belief they couldn't measure up.

Baldwin countered that there is "a very real problem in talking . . . about ethical considerations in a

society which is essentially not ethical." He acknowledged a willingness to "be one of the first Negroes
to be accepted either here or there," or to "wait ten
years or a generation to be fitted into the American
civilization, or American society." There was a caveat:
"If I really felt that one could be fitted into it as it now
is, as it's now constituted." That was the rub. America
had failed to grapple with the problem at its root: it
was not the Negro who was the problem, but instead,
it was "the white people's problem" that neither Hook
nor Myrdal nor anyone else involved was prepared to
address.

Long before it was in vogue in the academy,
Baldwin insisted on seeing whiteness as a fault line
in American race. Baldwin argued that the German
refugees "who have gotten or not gotten preferential
treatment were nevertheless looked on by the bulk of
the American community as white people" and never
served the same function as black folk. They were not,
as were Negroes, a source of cheap labor—which "allowed white people to say they were free . . . allowed
them to assume they were rich." Negroes built railroads and picked cotton for free. They made an economy that would be quite different without black labor.
"After all, part of the reason there is a battle going on
in the Deep South . . . is that as the Negro starts voting and becomes economically free, the power of the
Southern oligarchy will obviously be broken."

As for preferential treatment, Baldwin said that it was irrelevant if Negro kids were sent to a school for the gifted, or whether they were taught ethics and morality there. (This was to counter Hook's argument that one shouldn't increase the number of Negro students in schools for the gifted in order to achieve equity.) Baldwin noted that these Negro students would be sent back into a world in which those principles didn't prevail.

> What I am trying to say is that you can't hope to invest a child with a morality in school which is going to be destroyed in the streets of Harlem. Until we can deal with the question of *why* Negroes are kept in ghettos and why white men move out when Negroes move in; until we can deal with the question of *why* precisely in a free country we allow the South to dictate to the federal government; until we face our responsibilities as citizens of this country quite apart from the Negro problem, I don't see that we can begin to talk about the Negro problem with any hope of clarity.

Throughout the roundtable discussion, Baldwin anticipated many of the ideas that it would take most scholars another generation to explore, like his views on whiteness; the ability to speak with eloquence about the difference between immigrants and the enslaved; the political economy of the ghetto; the link between social theory and pedagogy; moral philosophy and its relationship to race; the reading of history from beneath, from the eyes of its victims; and intersectional social analysis. Baldwin's contributions on this score often were and continue to be missed because Baldwin's speech was refreshingly absent of jargon, and he labored hard to explain his beliefs in ordinary language.

Baldwin didn't write sociological treatises like W.E.B. Du Bois, or ethnographic studies like Zora Neale Hurston. His forte was the essay—the long developing, deeply personal rumination on the psychic and cultural status of his people and the moral and spiritual health of our nation. The way he plumbed the American soul has lasted precisely because it is rooted in issues that are, tragically, evergreen. In some ways, black life didn't matter much then, and doesn't matter much now. Police batons still flail black flesh; police bullets still unjustly riddle black bodies. Whiteness continues to metastasize across the body politic like a cancer that only goes into remission, sporadically, under the radiating prose and edifying action of a prophet.

Baldwin's critics couldn't make up their minds if he was not black enough or too black. "On one side of town I was an Uncle Tom," Baldwin said in a 1984 interview in *The Paris Review,* "and on the other the Angry Young Man."[7]

To be fair, Baldwin was not immune to the tendency of writers and thinkers to war with each other. He had eviscerated his mentor and benefactor Richard Wright in print in 1955—attacking *Native Son* as "a continuation, a complement of that monstrous legend it was written to destroy." It was only after Wright's death that Baldwin made amends of sorts in his moving essay, "Alas, Poor Richard." An exchange between prominent writers of the day sheds light on such disagreements. "Jimmy Baldwin couldn't write badly if he tried," Arna Bontemps wrote in a letter to his fellow poet Langston Hughes on January 26, 1961. "His piece on Dick [Richard Wright] seems deeply felt and has the ring of truth, but the account Dick gave me of their encounters was quite different." A few days later, Bontemps wrote to Hughes about what he termed literary falling outs. "Sometimes I think they are sort of ritualistic. The young writer makes a pilgrimage, meets the great-name writer, lingers till the spell wears off, then as the final act disagrees or quarrels with his deity."[8]

In the later 1960s younger writers like LeRoi Jones hammered Baldwin as irrelevant, while writer and Black Panther leader Eldridge Cleaver disparaged him as dangerous. Baldwin confined his criticism of Wright to the realm of ideas, but the younger writers ventured into more personal territory, assailing Baldwin as the wrong kind of man. Cleaver's venom toward Baldwin was by far the most troubling. His writing is the very definition of what is now termed "toxic masculinity." Cleaver's views were rooted in a rigid conception of manhood that cast any hint of homosexuality as a betrayal of racial politics. "There is in James Baldwin's work the most grueling, agonizing, total hatred of the blacks, particularly of himself, and the most shameful, fanatical, fawning, sycophantic love of the whites that one can find in the writings of any black American writer of note in our time," Cleaver said. "The case of James Baldwin aside for a moment, it seems that many Negro homosexuals, acquiescing in this racial death-wish, are outraged and frustrated because in their sickness they are unable to have a baby by a white man."[9]

Baldwin's response showed a big-mindedness that eluded many of his acerbic detractors. He wrote of meeting Cleaver and liking him before reading the Black Panther's malevolent diatribe. Baldwin said he didn't like it when he read it, but "I thought I could see why he felt compelled to issue what was, in fact, a warning: he was being a zealous watchman on the city wall, and I don't say that with a sneer." Baldwin said that Cleaver viewed him as "a dangerously odd, badly twisted, and fragile reed, of too much use to the

Establishment to be trusted by blacks." Baldwin wrote that Cleaver "uses my public reputation against me both naively and unjustly," and that he had confused Baldwin with "all those faggots, punks, and sissies, the sight and sound of whom, in prison, must have made him vomit more than once." Baldwin admitted, "I *am* an odd quantity. So is Eldridge; so are we all."[10] Baldwin's self-hatred is nearly as ugly as Cleaver's homophobic tirade, although it didn't keep him from appreciating the competing roles of intellectuals and revolutionaries.

> It is a pity that we won't, probably, ever have the time to attempt to define once more the relationship of the odd and disreputable artist to the odd and disreputable revolutionary; for the revolutionary, however odd, is rarely disreputable in the same way that an artist can be. These two seem doomed to stand forever at an odd and rather uncomfortable angle to each other, and they both stand at a sharp and not always comfortable angle to the people they both, in their different fashion, hope to serve.

Baldwin highlights again the unavoidable alienation the intellectual feels even from the community she claims to represent.

* * *

In a profile of Ta-Nehisi Coates published in the *New York Times* in September of 2017, right before Coates' forty-second birthday, Concepción de León writes about his meteoric rise following the publication of *Between the World and Me* in 2015:

> Toni Morrison, . . . strongly endorsed the book, calling it "required reading" and likening Mr. Coates to James Baldwin. That year, Mr. Coates was awarded a MacArthur Fellowship and the National Book Award in nonfiction. His appearances filled auditoriums and the book was adopted on college syllabuses. It has sold 1.5 million copies internationally and has been translated into 19 languages [making him] one of the most influential black intellectuals of his generation, joining predecessors including Ms. Morrison, Professor Henry Louis Gates, Jr., and Dr. Cornel West.[11]

Since the publication of his game-altering memoir, Coates has often uneasily but no less effectively worn the crown of America's foremost writer and public intellectual. But the most obvious point of the titanic curiosity that greeted Coates' *Between the World and Me* may also be its most overlooked: across the nation, in parlors and schoolrooms, in restaurants and train stations, on television and radio, in churches and barbershops, in newspapers and on social media, the nation was talking, all at once, finally, about a black man's *book*. Not his death, thank God; we were talking instead about his willful and unapologetic act of grand literacy. I am of a generation that still takes pride in extraordinary accomplishments by black folk. And recently few accomplishments have been bigger than this: a young man who uses words to expose the extravagant hoax of whiteness has also won a hearing among some of its most stubborn beneficiaries. It is remarkable to call a spade a spade, so to speak, when it comes to white identity; it is more remarkable to be caught doing that and to get away with it, and not just that, but to prosper in ungluing the artifice of race with a blowtorch.

Of course, he is not the first to do this; his most obvious predecessor, one he is conscious of, one he aimed for, is Baldwin. Some have taken offense to the comparison, proffered, mind you, by no less a literary light than the greatest living black writer, arguably the greatest ever: Toni Morrison. When Morrison brought Coates into Baldwin's orbit, she wasn't suggesting that they write sentences alike; they don't. Baldwin exults in luxurious, labyrinthine punctuation. A grammatical diagnosis of a Baldwin paragraph reveals a sublime congestion of commas that control the velocity of meaning, and a splatter of colons, semicolons, and dashes that support more dependent clauses than a serial monologist. Coates' lines are cleaner, simpler, gliding on the speed of graceful modifiers and sublime analogies; he also limns his meaning with pithy bursts of self-contained description. They are both beautiful styles. What they share, and what I believe Morrison meant in the comparison, is a forensic, analytical, cold-eyed stare-down of white moral innocence. And the concomitant insistence that we awaken from the fantasies, and swear off the myths, of what may be termed the *Imago Caucasi*—the collective white imagination that has made the world, or at least this country, in its image.

The James Baldwin comparison got up the dander of assorted high-brow types and Baldwin defenders; renunciations abounded. Is it bad to want to be like Baldwin? When one wants to be great why not emulate the greatest? LeBron James wants to be a greater basketball player than Michael Jordan and Kobe Bryant? Beautiful—we are the beneficiaries of the effort. Serena Williams wants her name in tennis to shine even brighter than that of Steffi Graf? Bravo. Kendrick Lamar wants us to mention his name with Nas and Jay-Z? In a word: Damn! Literary ambition is a good thing, or else what's a prose heaven for? Coates did a daring thing: he took Baldwin's conceit from the first and briefest section of *The Fire Next Time,* a letter penned to Baldwin's nephew, waged a bet that the American public could absorb even more of the epistolary device, and wrote a book-length essay to his son.

Some have claimed that because Coates isn't an activist, he dare not aspire to Baldwin's mantle, or even seek to emulate his eloquence. (Let's not forget that even Martin Luther King, Jr., dissed Baldwin when he declared he wasn't a Negro leader and that it was the press that had dubbed him a Negro spokesman.) But are we that literal?

Coates need not ever speak at a rally to be heard there, especially by those who are fed by his ravenous intellect and who drink in his considerable insight. His writings compose a powerful moral force for good; his words aid a thinking populace seeking ethical orientation and justifications for action. Coates' essay on reparations, collected in his *We Were Eight Years in Power: An American Tragedy,* summed up public policy and rigorous social scientific research on poverty and housing; he gave literary legs to an idea that walked right into the minds and mouths of folk who had previously spurned the concept or dismissed its relevance. He has battled on the Internet noted liberal thinker Jonathan Chait about the culture of poverty; vanquished conservative writer Shelby Steele in debate on television; and *Between the World and Me* caused talented *New York Times* columnist David

Brooks to fret out loud about his whiteness. How much more of a Baldwin figure need Coates be?

The truth is that it might be difficult for Baldwin to be James Baldwin now. His Herculean elegance may be lauded, but how well read in Baldwin are his fiercest defenders and newest advocates? It takes philosophical patience, and a universe of references spotted, looked up, traced, and then applied, to understand Baldwin's scope. Twitteracy doesn't necessarily encourage that sort of patience.

Coates is an enormously gifted writer who, while feeding his hunger to tell the truth about race, has also fed a nation starving for that same truth. He stands out in our day, as he might have stood out in an earlier time, because he is a curious man with a searching intellect and an eloquent pen.

The harsh criticism of Baldwin by Cruse and Cleaver is mirrored in our day by public intellectual Cornel West's bitter criticism of younger thinkers, most recently Coates. For several decades, West enjoyed status as a widely sought-after speaker and highly visible television commentator on race. The rise of the Internet, and the democratization of intellectual expression through digital literacy, has encouraged the proliferation of talented figures and new voices across the country. Coates symbolized a new cohort of digital intelligentsia who seized the reins of public criticism of race and forged a credible source of reflection and commentary that influenced political and cultural elites. In that light, West's criticisms of Coates reveal an almost deliberate misreading of Baldwin as witness and critic. As a major intellectual addressing race in America, West's views matter, as does his tragic decline, which is a cautionary tale of generational anxiety and the bitterness provoked by the fear of displacement.

West took strong exception to Morrison's argument that Coates was one of the figures taking up Baldwin's writerly vocation. West said that Morrison was wrong, that "Baldwin was a great writer of profound courage who spoke truth to power," but that "Coates is a clever wordsmith with journalistic talent who avoids any critique of the Black president in power."[12] West argues that "Baldwin's painful self-examination led to collective action and a focus on social movements." Coates, on the other hand, is possessed of a "fear-driven self-absorption [that] leads to individual escape and flight to safety." He accuses Coates of being "cowardly silent on the marvelous new militancy in Ferguson, Baltimore, New York, Oakland, Cleveland and other places." West says that Coates possesses the potential for growth, but that "without an analysis of capitalist wealth inequality, gender domination, homophobic degradation, Imperial occupation (all concrete forms of plunder) and collective fightback (not just personal struggle) Coates will remain a mere darling of White and Black Neo-liberals, paralyzed by their Obama worship and hence a distraction from the necessary courage and vision we need in our catastrophic times."

West offers the names of folk he thinks deserving of the sort of corporate media attention Coates receives, folk like "Robin D. G. Kelley, Imani Perry, Gerald Horne, [and] Eddie Glaude."

Most of what West said is patently false—Coates has written about Ferguson, Baltimore, and other flashpoints of police violence against unarmed black folk; he analyzed "capitalist wealth inequality" in his essay on reparations; he expressed admiration for many of the past black freedom-fighting greats; he has criticized Obama in a principled fashion while grappling with the forces that propelled and constrained him. West renewed his attack on Coates with the publication of Coates' *We Were Eight Years in Power,* making some of the same accusations and adding that Coates is plagued by "apolitical pessimism" as the "neoliberal face of the black freedom struggle."[13] West writes from his perch at Harvard, a university that is the very embodiment of neoliberal thought.

This is not the first time West has peppered prominent black thinkers and politicians with ad hominem assaults dressed up as ideological difference. He also accused Melissa Harris-Perry of being the darling of the liberal elite. He claimed that Al Sharpton served time as a boss on Obama's plantation. He accused Jesse Jackson of being addicted to television cameras. And he's accused me of being a sellout, prostitute, and bootlicker who's turned his back on the poor. What is behind West's animus? And how does it reflect the fierce and ugly tensions that rose in black America when the first black president took office? Amidst the enormous pride and psychological satisfaction many black folk felt in Obama's rise, it was exceedingly difficult to engage him with anything like the critical analysis warranted by his historic presidency.

* * *

West expresses great disdain for anyone he perceives as insufficiently tough on Barack Obama. He has accused Obama of political minstrelsy, calling him a "Rockefeller Republican in blackface,"[14] taunted him as a "brown-faced Clinton,"[15] and derided him as a "neoliberal opportunist." Despite West's disapproval of Obama, he eventually endorsed the political phenomenon. The two publicly embraced at a 2007 Apollo Theater fundraiser in Harlem during which West christened Obama "my brother . . . companion and comrade."[16] Obama praised West as "a genius, a public intellectual, a preacher, an oracle," and "a loving person."

In 1993, at the age of 39—around the same age that Baldwin and Coates made their splash—West catapulted to fame with the publication of his best-known work, *Race Matters*. It isn't a scholarly book, per se, although its pages carry the weight of his formidable intellect as he traces the cultural dynamics of race with exquisite and uncharacteristic—for the time—lucidity. (Dense jargon was at its zenith in the postmodernist academy of the 1990s.) *Race Matters* changed how we speak of black identity in the United States. It gave our country a golden pun for matters of race that mattered more than they should. West's rise brought great satisfaction: one of the smartest men of his generation also became one of its most popular.

The intellectual landscape had shifted dramatically beneath West's feet by the time Obama went after the presidency. If West's most notable book argued that race mattered, his celebrity and iconic status meant that his endorsement also mattered. West remained allied with Obama until he took the White House and, in football parlance, faked left and ran right. "[Obama] posed as a progressive and turned out to be counterfeit," West complained in an interview with *Salon*. "He acted as if he was . . . concerned about the issues of serious injustice and inequality, and it turned out that he's just another neoliberal centrist with a smile and with a nice rhetorical flair."[17]

Some critics, and I am among them, have held Obama's feet to the fire about his tepid interventions on behalf of beleaguered black folk.[18] What we have not done is make the attacks personal, as has West, or drape contempt in the cloth of ideological dispute. "I would rather have a white president fundamentally dedicated to eradicating poverty and enhancing the plight of working people than a black president tied to Wall Street and drones," he told *The Guardian*.[19]

West believed himself personally betrayed by Obama because of his (supposed) disinterest after the election. It is a sad truth that most politicians are serial rhetorical lovers and promiscuous ideological mates, leaving behind scores of briefly valued surrogates and supporters. But West felt spurned and was embittered.

The role of the intellectual is to deepen inquiry and broaden understanding. In *Brother West,* West admitted that he is "more a natural reader than natural writer," adding that "writing requires a concerted effort and forced discipline," but that he reads "as easily as I breathe."[20] I can say with certainty, as a college professor for the last quarter century, that most of my students feel the same way! What's more, West's off-the-cuff riffs and rants, spoken into a microphone and later transcribed to the page, lack the discipline of the written word. West's rhetorical genius is undeniable, but there are limits on what speaking can do for someone trying to wrestle angels or battle demons to the page. This is no biased preference for the written word over the spoken; I am far from a champion of a Eurocentric paradigm of literacy. This is about scholar versus talker. Improvisational speaking bears its wonders: the emergence on the spot of turns of thought and pathways of insight one hadn't planned, and the rapturous discovery, in front of a live audience, of meanings that usually lie buried beneath the rubble of formal restrictions and literary conventions. Yet West's difficulty in writing is hugely confining. For scholars, there is a depth that can only be tapped through the rigorous reworking of the same sentences until the meaning comes clean—or as clean as one can make it.

The ecstasies of the spoken word, when scholarship is at stake, leave the deep reader and the long listener hungry for more. Writing is an often painful task that can feel like the death of one's past. Equally discomfiting is seeing one's present commitments to truths crumble once one begins to tap away at the keyboard or scar the page with ink. Writing demands a different sort of apprenticeship to ideas than does speaking. It beckons one to revisit over an extended, or at least delayed, period the same material and to revise what one thinks. Revision is reading again and again what one writes so that one can think again and again about what one wants to say and in turn determine if better and deeper things can be said.

West admires the Socratic process of questioning ideas and practices in fruitful dialogue, and while that may elicit thoughts he yearned to express anyhow, he's at the mercy of his interlocutors. Thus, when West inveighs, stampedes, and kvetches, he gets on a roll that might be amplified in conversation but arrested in print. It's not a matter of skillful editing, either, so that the verbal repetition and set pieces that orators depend on get clipped and swept aside with the redactor's broom. It's the conceptual framework that suffers in translating what's spoken to what's written, since writing is about contrived naturalness: rigging the system of meaning to turn out the way you want, and making it look normal and inevitable in the process.

An essential tenet of West's arguments about the worth and function of intellectuals is his belief about prophets, and more important, his claim to be one. "I am a prophetic Christian freedom fighter," West wrote in one essay, adding in his memoir, "I see my role as . . . someone who feels both a Socratic and prophetic calling."[21]

Prophets in the Judeo-Christian tradition draw on Divine inspiration to speak God's words on earth. Among black Americans, prophecy is often rooted in religious stories of overcoming oppression while influencing the moral vision of social activists. Black prophets like James Baldwin are highly esteemed because they symbolize black resistance to white supremacy, stoke insurgence against the suppression of our freedom, inspire combat against social and political oppression, and risk their lives in the service of their people and the nation's ideals. They remind us of the full measure of God's love for the weak and unprotected.

The argument over who and what is prophetic has rarely been more heated in black culture than it is now. The model of the charismatic black male leader has come in for deserved drubbing since it overlooks the contributions of women and children that often went unheralded in the civil rights movement and earlier black freedom struggles. Queer activists sparked the Black Lives Matter movement, underscoring the unacknowledged sacrifice of black folk who have often been confined to the closets and corners of black existence. Even those who enjoy a direct relationship to King and to Malcolm X haven't escaped scrutiny. Louis Farrakhan is faulted (and praised) for his distance from Malcolm's racial politics, and Jesse Jackson and Al Sharpton have been pilloried for lacking King's gravitas and grace. The truth of those assessments is not as important as the value of the comparison: it holds would-be prophets to account for standards of achievement both noble and nostalgic, real and imagined.

Despite the profusion of prophecy in his texts and talks, West has never bothered to tell us in rich detail what makes a person a prophet. In *Black Prophetic Fire,* West offered a sweeping assessment of contemporary black life: "Black people once put a premium on serving the community, lifting others, and finding joy in empowering others," he wrote. "Black people once had a strong prophetic tradition of lifting every voice."[22] Today, however, "Black people have succumbed to individualistic projects in pursuit of wealth, health, and status."

West's failure to carefully chart the history and ethical arc of prophecy leads him to wild overstatement. To paraphrase Supreme Court Justice Potter Stewart's famous definition of pornography, West may not seek to define a prophet, but he knows one when he sees one, and quite often, they sound just like him.

What makes West a prophet? Is it his willingness to call out corporate elites and assail the purveyors of injustice and inequality? The actor Russell Brand does that in his book *Revolution*. Is it West's self-identification with the poor? Tupac Shakur had that on lock. Is it West's self-styled resistance to police brutality, evidenced by his occasional willingness to get arrested in highly staged and camera-ready gestures of civil disobedience, such as in Ferguson in the fall of 2014? West sees King as a prophet, but Jackson and Sharpton, who have also courted arrest in public fashion, are "ontologically addicted to the camera."[23]

West most closely identifies with a black prophetic tradition that has deep roots in the church. But ordained ministers, and especially pastors, must give account to the congregations or denominations that offer them institutional support and the legitimacy to prophesize. They may face severe consequences—including excommunication, censorship, being defrocked, or even expelled from their parishes—for their acts. The words and prophetic actions of these brave souls impact their ministerial standing and their vocation.

As a freelancing, itinerant, nonordained, self-anointed prophet, West has only to answer to himself. That may symbolize a grand resistance to institutional authority, but it's also a failure to acknowledge the institutional responsibilities that religious prophets bear. Most ministers are clerics attending to the needs of the local parish. Only a select few are cut from prophetic cloth. Yet nearly all the religious figures we recognize as prophets—Adam Clayton Powell, Jr., King, Jackson, Sharpton—were ordained as ministers. Powell and King were pastors of local churches as well. To be sure, there are prophets who are not ministers or religious figures—especially women, whose path to the ministry has been blocked by sexist theologies—but most of them have ties to organizations or institutions that hold them accountable.

West might argue that not being ordained leaves him free to act on his prophetic instincts and even disagree with the church on social matters. Thus he avoids the negative consequences of ordination while remaining spiritually anchored. That's fine if you're a run-of-the-mill Christian, but there is, and should be, a higher standard for prophets. True prophets embrace religious authority and bravely stand up to it in the name of a higher power. One need not be Martin Luther King to qualify as a prophet. But when you claim to be a prophet, you are expected, as the classic gospel song goes, to live the life you sing about in your song.

West's lack of understanding of the prophetic tradition is perhaps most evident in his criticism of Sharpton and Jackson. He berates them for their appetite for access to power, their desire for insider status. Even if we concede for the moment that this is true, it isn't a failure of their prophecy but of West's ability to distinguish between kinds of prophets. In his 1995 book, *The Preacher King,* Duke Divinity School Professor Richard Lischer noted that in ancient Israel, the central prophet moved within the power structure, reminding the people of their covenant with God and also consulting kings on military matters and issues of national significance. Peripheral prophets were outsiders who embraced the poor, criticized the monarchy, and opposed war.

West ignores these variations, which results in an idealized, and deeply flawed, portrait of King as a peripheral prophet who was only useful when he hugged the margin. But that, Lischer argued, is a distorted rendering of King's prophetic profile.

> As a central prophet, Martin Luther King had been deeply involved with the Johnson administration's efforts to pass civil rights legislation. Beginning already in the Eisenhower administration and increasing steadily throughout the turbulent Kennedy years, he had been regularly consulted on matters of interest to the Negro in America. After the March on Washington, Kennedy had scrambled to align himself with King's beautifully articulated ideals. In some of Lyndon Johnson's early civil rights speeches, King was gratified to hear echoes of his own ideas. No black leader had ever enjoyed comparable access to the Oval Office and the power it represented.[24]

King moved from central to peripheral prophet in his last few years with an emphasis on economic justice and antiwar activism—views he grew into as he wrestled with his conscience, his staff, and the folk to whom he was accountable. But West's insistence that only peripheral prophets are genuine and powerful is undercut by the legislation King helped to pass as a central prophet: the Civil Rights Act and the Voting Rights Act. The Fair Housing Act of 1968 was quickly passed in his memory after his brutal assassination. King was arguably more beneficial to the folk he loved when he swayed power with his influence and vision. When West begrudged Sharpton his closeness to Obama, he ignored the fact that King had similar access.

Sharpton and Jackson eventually moved in the opposite prophetic direction of King. While King kissed the periphery with courageous vigor, Jackson, and especially Sharpton, started on the periphery before coming into their own on the inside. Jackson's rise was driven by King's assassination, and while forging alliances with other outsiders on the black left, he easily adapted to the role of the inside-outsider who identified with the downcast while making his way to the heart of the Democratic Party. Sharpton had to kill his periphery persona; the rabble-rousing and inflammatory style of his early days is gone.

If West's harangues against Obama are not the words of a prophet, then how do we account for his extravagant excoriations? They might be explained with a bit of the moral psychology West liked to apply to the former president. West said in 2011 that "my dear brother Barack Obama has a certain fear of free black men," because as a biracial child growing up in a white world, "he's always had to fear being a white man with black skin."[25] West said that when Obama "meets an independent black brother, it is frightening."

Yet Obama wasn't too frightened to confront West. According to Jonathan Alter's 2013 book, *The Center Holds: Obama and His Enemies,* at the 2010 National Urban League convention, Obama barked at West, "I'm not progressive? What kind of shit is this?" Other foul words were uttered, West added, and Obama "cussed me out."[26]

The irony is that, as highly charged as his criticism has become, West is, in some ways, not that different from Obama. The president had long wished to be the grand architect of bipartisanship, the conciliator of left and right, the bridge between conservatives and liberals. West used to fancy himself a similar figure; he sought to account for the suffering of black America by steering between the arguments of conservative behaviorists and liberal structuralists. He thought it was important to acknowledge self-inflicted injuries as well as dehumanizing forces. As Stephen Steinberg, a sociologist at Queens College, has argued, West set himself up as "the voice of reason and moderation between liberals and conservatives," as the "mediator between ideological extremes."[27] Obama similarly argued that black folk must cultivate moral excellence at home and in the community even as he admitted that the government must help fight black suffering.

West's prescription for what ails black folk—and a big part of Obama's plan, too—involves a personal and behavioral dimension beyond social or political change. For West, the cure is a politics of conversion fueled by a strong love ethic. "Nihilism is not overcome by arguments or analyses; it is tamed by love and care," West wrote in *Race Matters*. "Any disease of the soul must be conquered by a turning of one's soul. This turning is done through one's own affirmation of one's worth—an affirmation fueled by the concern for others."[28] West and Obama both advocated intervention for our most vulnerable citizens, but while West focuses on combating market forces that "edge out nonmarket values—love, care, service to others—handed down by preceding generations,"[29] Obama, as Alter contends, has been more practical: offering Pell grants; stimulus money that saved the jobs of hundreds of thousands of black state and local workers; the Fair Sentencing Act of 2010, which reduced the disparity of sentences for powdered and crack cocaine; the extension of the Earned Income Tax Credit, which kept millions of working poor blacks from sliding into poverty; and the extension of unemployment insurance and food stamps, which helped millions of blacks.

The odd thing is that Obama talked right—chiding personal irresponsibility in a way that presumed the pathology of many black families and neighborhoods—but veered left in his public policy. West, on the other hand, talks left but thinks right. In

Race Matters, West argued that the spiritual malady of "nihilism" is the greatest threat to black America—not racism, not class inequality, not material hardship or poverty or hyperincarceration. Steinberg says that despite "frequent caveats, West has succeeded in shifting the focus of blame onto the black community. The affliction is *theirs*—something we shall call 'nihilism.'" West did as much to slam the poor with his stylish, postmodern update of ghetto pathology and blame-the-victim reasoning as any conservative thinker. In a 2014 interview on HuffPost Live, then–Morehouse College professor Marc Lamont Hill challenged West about his attacks on his fellow black progressives. West compared himself to biblical prophets Jeremiah and Amos, contending there is "a certain intensity to prophetic language that hits deep and seems to be unfair, but is coming from a place of such righteous indignation." Not content to be in league with mere prophets, West compared himself with Christ and cast those who disagreed with him in the role of the Lord's unprincipled opponents. "If we could hear what Jesus was saying when he ran out the money changers in the temple, it was not polite discourse."

If this isn't the height of self-righteousness, it is the depth of delusion and exegetical corruption—isolating and then interpreting a text to sanctify his scurrilous views. But West's broadsides lack a crucial element. Lischer argued that late in his career King, too, "began to give full vent to his rage."[30] But un-like West, King's "was the holy rage of the prophetic tradition."

I think West's deep loathing of Obama draws on some profoundly personal energy that is ultimately irrational—it's a species of antipathy that no politi-cal difference could ever explain. The same can be said, sadly, for his beef with Ta-Nehisi Coates. When West attacked Coates on social media, his views were co-signed by white supremacist Richard Spencer, a shocking endorsement that drove Coates off social media. West has sacrificed friendships and cut ties with former comrades because he insists that only outright denunciation of Obama will do. It is a colossal loss for such a gifted man to surrender to unheroic truculence.

* * *

James Baldwin finished his reflections on Eldridge Cleaver with wise words:

> I think that it is just as well to remember that the people are one mystery and that the person is another. Though I know what a very bitter and delicate and dangerous conundrum this is, it yet seems to me that a failure to respect the person so dangerously limits one's percep-tion of the people that one risks betraying them

and oneself, either by sinking to the apathy of cynical disappointment, or rising to the rage of knowing, better than the people do, what the people want. Ultimately, the artist and the revolutionary function as they function, and pay whatever dues they must pay behind it because they are both possessed by a vision, and they do not so much follow this vision as find themselves driven by it. Otherwise, they could never endure, much less embrace, the lives they are compelled to lead. And I think we need each other, and have much to learn from each other, and, more than ever, now.[31]

* * *

If personal and ideological clashes shape combat between some thinkers, a different kind of debate informs the perspective of Erin Aubry Kaplan, who is part of a new generation of black female public intellectuals, thinkers who seem to be far more numerous, or at least far more visible, now than in Hansberry's day. If Ta-Nehisi Coates has rightly drawn praise for his Baldwinian ambitions, then Kaplan is due far more recognition for her Baldwinesque fusion of personal narrative and political reflection. Kaplan writes about black life and race amidst tensions between what may be termed absolutist and cosmopolitan critics. Afrocentric thinkers like Cheikh Anta Diop and Chancellor

Williams might be cast in the role of racial absolut-
ists, smart people arguing for a single explanation of
black culture's rise, it's extraordinary genius, for instance, or its ruin at the hands of white supremacy.
And critics like Zora Neale Hurston and Ralph Ellison
might be cast as racial cosmopolitans, astute observ-
ers of identity and culture whose skepticism about the
things we're supposed to know about race and blackness brings us closer than ever to finding the truth.
When it comes to race and blackness, Erin Aubry Kaplan is clearly in the cosmopolitan camp, playing the
role of a discerning critic of racial certainties and cultural absolutes.

It is poetically just that a writer of Kaplan's im-
mense gifts emerged to assume rhetorical weight and
do intellectual battle in the Age of Obama, both in her
book of essays, *Black Talk, Blue Thoughts, and Walking the Color Line,* and in her book *I Heart Obama.*
These were and are hard times for race. If Baldwin
approached identity with a ruthless clarity, allowing
the racial chips to fall where they may, Kaplan refuses
to blink her eyes or to pretend that we are living in
a post-racial nirvana where the former black occu-
pant of the White House loosed magical healing and
erased the nation's racial wound. Kaplan's meditation
on Obama is remarkable. It measures his stride across
the political landscape, fingerprints his influence
against the culture that at once adores and indicts

him, and empathizes with his huge difficulty in publicly identifying with black folk.

Yet Kaplan is instructive in her disappointment that Obama hadn't worked harder to achieve such identification. His failure of nerve meant that he often got manipulative and dismissive by turns, whether handling racial episodes like his administration's abortive firing of agricultural department official Shirley Sherrod or his stoic inattention to record levels of black unemployment. Kaplan beautifully narrates the Obama two-step: he appeared to dance with black folk, with black interests, with black culture, only to abandon us as we hungered for the tamest reciprocity and the feeblest gesture of support. Black folk may have expected Alvin Ailey's *Revelations* but ended up instead with Darren Aronofsky's *Black Swan*.

Kaplan brings sharp intelligence to pop culture and politics. While Baldwin and Coates feel the world through their male vibrations, Kaplan fingers with distinctive percussiveness the gender grain of black experience. Few have pleaded as eloquently for the right shade of makeup in a culture that is still color-struck in every way except any that help the complexions or egos of black women. Kaplan is soulful, yet analytical, about the problems that grab at the black female bottom. In fact, she has the sort of knowledge of her subject that philosophers call, drolly enough, "a posteriori," that is, knowledge grounded in experience and empirical evidence. Kaplan's butt becomes exhibit A, and, as she lets on, she's got ample evidence to carry her argument about the black behind's splendors and trials. Kaplan also questions racial orthodoxies and the certainties of black life with irresistible logic, like some kinder, gentler Thurgood Marshall pressing for the truth of our culture under the oaths we swear by. Kaplan artfully examines the pressure to be positive in black life, and to barely acknowledge the vast sadness that clouds us into silent solidarity, a depression she bravely exposes in the first person.

Kaplan's courage is impressive because, as she notes, black artists are usually only allowed to form public identities. Private identities are off limits, the opposite of white artists who shape the larger world around their intimate reflections. In an essay ostensibly on songwriter Randy Newman, Kaplan offers a precedent, perhaps even a justification, for rappers who refer to themselves in the third person. "Hov did that so hopefully you won't have to go through that," Jay-Z raps about his drug-dealing days. His statement is trebly resonant: it's the third-person reference to the artist Shawn Carter, whose pen name Jay-Z is suggested by yet another alias, "Hov," itself short for "Hova," the shortened version of Jehovah, meant to suggest Carter's god-like skills on the mic. While Kaplan didn't intend an extended riff on the literary identities encouraged in hip hop—though she offers sophisticated spins on what hip hop makes of the world in several spots—her highly allusive work invites us to see the connections. But that's the case throughout *Black Talk, Blue Thoughts, and Walking the Color Line*—Kaplan clarifies a lot more than what she aims to make clear. It's one of the surest marks of her fertile intelligence and a certain sign of her well-earned spot in the pantheon of luminaries to which Baldwin and Coates belong.

Kaplan is open to a wide range of ideas when it comes to black culture even as she eschews the rah-rah racial fundamentalism of strictly positive thinking. It's not that Kaplan doesn't get the need for black folk to combat negativity; her adroit dismantling of *our* habit of collecting mammies and other racially charged curios makes it clear that she thinks something bad has a hold on us, and it may just be that *we* won't let Pharaoh go—that is, the thing that enslaves or defeats us—or loosen our grip on the images that stereotype us, like Uncle Ben or Aunt Jemima. But Kaplan knows that even if we could completely disown our fictive kin from the nation's racist past our problems wouldn't go away. (Exactly whose aunt and uncle are they anyway?) The cooning has gone high-tech and the stereotypes have migrated from the rice box to the "idiot box" and are now broadcast in high definition. That's why Kaplan defiantly refuses to amplify the clamor for more black faces on television:

more isn't necessarily better. Her luminous doubt and principled skepticism serves her well in battling an absolutist race theory.

The best deterrent to black buffoonery is black brilliance—but a brilliance that serves what's complex about black life more than what's positive. This is where Kaplan's Baldwinian pedigree shines brightly. Kaplan shows that the most useful way to define black culture is in contrasting the simple and the complex. She makes it plain that getting caught up in the cult of opposition to the "negative" is not only imperfect (your negative could be my positive, as glimpsed in matters as diverse as styles of dress or sexual orientation), but it's often downright destructive. Bill Cosby's war against the poor was dressed up as a positive attempt to spread bootstrap wit and to get the poor to help themselves. But Kaplan deftly reveals how Cosby's comprehension simply wasn't big enough to match the bruising and bewildering complexity of black life. Sometimes it's what Kaplan doesn't say that's most intriguing. Her take on Magic Johnson's populist entrepreneurialism never once uses the word hustle, but her essay skillfully parses the many ways the word can be applied: Magic's hustle as a player, the hustle he'd acquired when he was forced by illness to retire from basketball, his hustle to nobly serve the inner city, and politicians who tried to hustle Magic and ended up getting hustled themselves.

Kaplan's complicated view covers a generous swath of black life: interracial relations, family dynamics, genetic inheritance, educational aspirations, generational tensions, political conflicts, vistas of celebrity, the lure of neighborhood and geography, and the varied lessons of sports. Kaplan's take on Tiger Woods, or better yet, her being fully taken by Tiger, ambushed by a near total devotion to him, where the heroic and erotic merge, written a full decade before his self-immolation, shows how it was easy for Tiger to give in to the vast female adoration that surrounded him. Kaplan squeezes great insight from the controversy over Serena Williams' racy catsuit—and how gloriously it clung to the tennis star's beautifully sculpted physique. Serena's ongoing bravura knocks all parties from their respective comfort zones, while her unruffled demeanor is part of a racial etiquette that prescribes behavior rather than protests limits. There's revolution in her backhand.

Kaplan is a superb stylist and a new master of the essay, which means, at least in the black literary tradition she embraces, that she, too, is a superb moralist like her predecessors Ellison and Baldwin, and Walker, Hurston, and Morrison as well. That's not a haphazard list, either, as Kaplan taps a vein composed of these scribes. She makes use of Ellison's broad learning and analytical acuity, and his grasp of the folkways and mores of black culture. Baldwin's redemptive eloquence and his moral outrage at the blasts on black humanity. Walker's humane lyricism in defense of vulnerable folk. Hurston's ethnographic scrupulousness in limning black existence. And Morrison's keen eye for the horrors that can only be tamed by resilient black imagination. Kaplan's resonant, luminous prose sings the black body eclectic.

Kaplan's complex, allusive, elegant essays are a reminder of what we are made of, and what we can achieve, in a time of racial uncertainty. But she is no distant observer; she is part of all that she has met. She is dissatisfied with how things are, and in no mood to be shallowly optimistic. Through her work she finds, and offers to us, a deeper virtue than optimism: a hope born of triumph over the despotic sway of bigotry and ignorance. It is not rooted in romantic notions of race. Neither does it depend on the willful denial of race in the public square. It echoes in the effort to tell as much of the truth as possible about the condition of black folk and the state of race in America and to let that truth outshine all our fantasies and fears.

* * *

Black intellectuals have often been far more colorful and combative than stereotypes of their cloistered ivory tower existence suggest. If nothing else, their clashes and conflicts reveal a hunger for change and justice that often drives black thinkers to the very abyss they brilliantly describe and warn others to avoid. Beyond their heated disagreements and their bitter disputes, black intellectuals diagnose and confront racial catastrophes and political crises in a fashion that helps those who take action against these ills gain a better sense of what is at stake—with a surer grasp of the troubles that must be quelled and the solutions that must be found if we are to thrive and overcome.

THE ACTIVISTS 1

POLICY AND WITNESS

B lack activism has existed as long as the white world has viewed black folk as inferior. Black activists have often upset the establishment by demanding justice for the vulnerable and beleaguered—from the enslaved preacher Nat Turner, who led a rebellion to set his people free, to Black Lives Matter protesters interrupting business as usual to seek redress for victims of police brutality.

Bobby Kennedy got angry at Jimmy Baldwin and his friends because he thought they were ignorant of the law, ignorant of what he and his brother had been trying to do to improve race relations, and more interested in witness than policy. Their volatile exchange was a watershed moment in American politics, revealing the limits of liberal goodwill and the explosive power of truth through testimony.

It was the beginning of a disagreement that still rages today: Do black activists seek to improve black life through policies that translate the intent of politics, or does improvement come through the ethical force of witness? Does racial progress happen when black activists appeal to the government for change, or is it sparked by their efforts outside the system? And what happens when black activists cling tenaciously to ideologies that ultimately undermine the political fortunes of the people they claim to represent? Even though there are striking differences between 1963 and our day, these questions linger and continue to shape our perceptions of race.

* * *

When Kennedy and Baldwin met in 1963, public schools, transportation, and restaurants in the South were segregated. The masses of black folk in the region could not vote. Even though President Kennedy had stalled on civil rights legislation, he threw black folk a bone here and there—standing with James Meredith as he integrated the University of Mississippi and bailing out jailed Freedom Riders in Alabama. The Kennedys were trying to win elections while accommodating social change.

Baldwin and his activist friends believed that elections were useless if they didn't address the social issues that politics aimed to resolve. Policy didn't necessarily challenge the racist and classist assumptions that denied black folk their humanity. Witness would validate black humanity. Bobby tried to get off easy in demanding the change of law; Baldwin's aim was something loftier still—a change of what French political scientist Alexis de Tocqueville called the "habits of the heart" so that American democracy could be transformed by spirit as much as by politics.

"Bobby didn't understand what we were trying to tell him," Baldwin said.

> He didn't understand our urgency. For him it was a political matter. It was a matter of finding out what's wrong in the twelfth ward and correcting it . . . like packages or whatever the kids wanted in the twelfth ward, giving it to them and everything would be all right. But what was wrong in the twelfth ward in this case turned out to be something very sinister, very deep, that couldn't be solved in the usual way . . . And our apprehension of his misunderstanding made it very tense, and finally very ugly. If we couldn't make the Attorney General of the United States, who was a fairly young and intelligent man, understand the urgency of the black situation, there wasn't any hope at all.[1]

It is not that Baldwin and his activist cohort disavowed the hard and necessary work of shaping policies that responded to black need, policies that would offer the social goods black folk deserved. It is that they saw public policy without personal witness as an insufficient spur to genuine social change. This is why Baldwin's crew insisted that President Kennedy see race as a *moral* issue and not simply a political one. Legislation and public policy would surely solve many of the practical problems black folk confronted, but they could hardly address the deep investment in black inferiority, or white innocence, that attended the debate on race in America. Bobby resisted witness because it would require that he fundamentally change the way he saw himself in relation to black people.

Baldwin and his activist friends demanded that Bobby witness them, that he actually hear the rage he claimed to want to understand. They forced him to reject the white supremacist beliefs that hobbled even policies meant to relieve black suffering. It was tough for a white liberal to hear that the urge to help may be part of the problem, especially if that urge was fueled by condescension and ignorance of black life. Baldwin had spoken with furious eloquence about the animus to blackness that haunted the American soul. Baldwin understood that policy could never make white people think differently. The perception of black people often shapes how and when the law is applied. The moral dimensions of race exert a profound influence on how we distribute social goods, apply public policy and laws, and determine the worth and value of human life. It is already against the law for the police to unjustly murder black folk.

In a way, *The Fire Next Time* had a better chance of conveying the hurt and trauma of black life than a compelling brief by legendary lawyer Thurgood Marshall, or even a speech as eloquent as "I Have a Dream" by Martin Luther King, Jr. Baldwin personalized the quest for justice. In the black freedom struggle, sociology was often tied to autobiography, politics to prophecy. Baldwin often used the collective personal pronoun "I" to represent the race in a way that collapsed past and present: "I picked the cotton and I carried it to market and I built the railroads under someone else's whip," he stated in a debate with William F. Buckley at Cambridge University in 1965.[2]

Kennedy spurned the emotionalism of the activists gathered before him; he deplored their testifying and witnessing and orating, all of which seemed hysterical. They in turn deemed Kennedy laughable in the effort to fix what was wrong with black folk without listening to them, *even after* he asked what they saw and needed. When they spoke in an emotional and personal way, Kennedy dismissed them as plagued by guilt, and mocked them as off-kilter or desperate to prove their street credibility. If Bobby couldn't hear them, how could he possibly hear millions of Negroes who were even angrier and more hurt?

Kennedy may have been sore at Baldwin and his activist crew for refusing to talk policy, but it's not as if he lacked recommendations for sweeping legislation from other Negro activists and leaders. The NAACP offered legal remedies for what ailed black folk; Kenneth Clark teamed up with them to use his expertise to suggest ways to defeat Jim Crow in public schools. When leaders like King pressed the Kennedys on voting rights, they balked at such legislation. Black leaders pushed to see the enforcement of *Brown v. Board of Education* sped up, with the political wind of the administration behind their backs, but Jack Kennedy preferred letting Negroes see movies in a theater, which seemed a natural right to the president, rather than forcing white kids to sit next to Negroes and learn, which didn't.

* * *

If Robert Kennedy really wanted to talk policy, then he would have spoken to Roy Wilkins or Whitney Young. Or to Martin Luther King, Jr., arguably the greatest activist in the nation's history. Both Baldwin and Bobby had close but complicated relationships with King. Baldwin's relationship with the foremost civil rights leader was often warm, but just as often laced with tensions from each end: King admired

Baldwin but also kept distance between them because of his feeling that Baldwin's deeply poetic rhetorical gestures reeked of his queer identity, and besides, he viewed the writer as more of a spokesman than a true leader.

Baldwin greatly admired King but knew that there were limitations to what he might say about race because he led an organization that held him accountable.

Perhaps this is why Baldwin claimed not to have invited Martin to their meeting; he wanted folk there who spoke from their own personal conviction, and not for a group, and so didn't feel the need to censor themselves. "I didn't want Martin there," Baldwin said afterward. "[Kennedy had] already talked to Martin," who "had to speak for the Southern Christian Leadership Conference, whereas none of us was speaking for any organization."[3] But Kenneth Clark says Baldwin had reached out to King, who couldn't come because he was tied up in Chicago and instead deputized Clark to speak for him.

"Kenneth, you have my proxy," King said.

King's presence hovered over the meeting, if for no other reason than, by the time it was done, King emerged clearly for Kennedy as the sort of leader one could talk to about policy issues and get some sound advice, even if one didn't always follow that advice. In 1961 Bobby had a tense phone exchange with King over the Freedom Riders when Kennedy wanted to

bail them out of jail in Jackson, Mississippi, and King
said they'd stay in jail to further highlight injustice.

> KING: It's a matter of conscience and morality.
> They must use their lives and their bodies to
> right a wrong.
>
> KENNEDY: This is not going to have the slight-
> est effect on what the government is going
> to do in this field or any other. The fact that
> they stay in jail is not going to have the
> slightest effect on me.
>
> KING: Perhaps it would help if students came
> down here by the hundreds—by the hun-
> dreds of thousands.
>
> KENNEDY: The country belongs to you as much
> as to me. You can determine what's best just
> as well as I can, but don't make statements
> that sound like a threat. That's not the way
> to deal with us.
>
> [A silence]
>
> KING: It's difficult to understand the position
> of oppressed people. Ours is a way out—
> creative, moral and nonviolent. It is not tied
> to black supremacy or Communism but to
> the plight of the oppressed. It can save the
> soul of America. You must understand that
> we've made no gains without pressure and

> I hope that pressure will always be moral,
> legal and peaceful.

KENNEDY: But the problem won't be settled in
Jackson, Mississippi, but by strong federal
action.

KING: I'm deeply appreciative of what the
administration is doing. I see a ray of hope,
but I am different than my father. I feel the
need of being free now!

KENNEDY: Well, it all depends on what you and
the people in jail decide. If they want to get
out, we can get them out.

KING: They'll stay.[4]

Even on their call, Bobby was defensive about King's statement that the young activists would put their bodies on the line for justice, as the attorney general insisted that he wouldn't be moved by their show of conscience. Kennedy may have been nostalgic for speaking with leaders like King after his bruising encounter with Baldwin's group, but it wasn't because he was willing to offer King any more than he seemed prepared to offer Baldwin.

In the fall of 1962 Baldwin and King sat up into the wee hours of the morning in a train station in Boston after President Kennedy gave a speech explaining the effort to get James Meredith registered at the University of Mississippi in Oxford—after the

racist governor duplicitously dithered and Kennedy finally had to send in the troops. Baldwin and King de-
spaired over the events. Historian William Goldsmith
sat with the legendary duo, and he recalled, it "was
not only the clumsiness and hesitancy with which the
whole business was handled that depressed them, but
the lack of moral conviction in the President's remarks
as he spoke patronizingly of war heroes and football
stars to the rioting students and yahoos in Oxford that
awful Sunday night."[5] Baldwin and King concluded
that it was "the wrong speech, to the wrong group, in
the wrong tone, at the wrong time."

King certainly knew about the right words at the
right time for the right occasion. Less than a year later,
he would make his electrifying oratorical debut on the
national stage with "I Have a Dream." August 28, 1963,
was his moment to soar. Baldwin was right there to
see for himself, just as he had journeyed to Montgomery early in King's ministry, after his victorious boy-
cott, to hear what all the commotion was about.

> King is a great speaker. The secret of his great-
> ness does not lie in his voice or his presence
> or his manner, though it has something to do
> with all these; nor does it lie in his verbal range
> or felicity, which are not striking; nor does he
> have any capacity for those stunning, dema-
> gogic flights of the imagination which bring

an audience cheering to its feet. The secret lies,
I think, in his intimate knowledge of the people
he is addressing, be they black or white, and
in the forthrightness with which he speaks of
those things which hurt and baffle them. He
does not offer any easy comfort and this keeps
his hearers absolutely tense. He allows them
their self-respect—indeed, he insists on it.[6]

But despite King's enormous gifts, Bobby Kennedy didn't want to hear from him or any of the other civil rights stalwarts, leaders, and activists.

* * *

There was a price to pay for calling on figures outside of black leadership circles: one would have to hear unvarnished truths in ways white ears—especially of those in positions of power—were unaccustomed to. When Bobby heard the truth he couldn't bear it. Policy at that point was a refuge from the truth.

The two needs weren't ultimately incompatible; witness might fuel the aspiration to reshape public policy to lessen the suffering of the black masses. If Kennedy deemed Baldwin's group disruptive—Baldwin admitted, after all, they were a "fairly rowdy, independent, tough-minded [gathering of] men and women"[7]—it should be remembered that the civil rights movement shocked the American system.

Martin Luther King may have a statue in his memory on the National Mall, but the FBI considered him "the most dangerous Negro" in America. His fellow activists were hosed, beaten, bitten by dogs, even murdered—sometimes with the help of law enforcement, more often as they looked the other way in cruel indifference. Black witness was an affront to American denial, the black bid for equality salt in the ongoing wound of Confederate loss.

Jimmy and his activist friends were there to tell Bobby about the suffering that had scarred each black person in that room; that had scarred or killed people they loved; that had buried their communities in poverty; that had withheld their right to vote; that had lynched their grandfathers, raped their grandmothers, set the dogs on their children, called them "nigger" for daring to sit at a lunch counter; that had tried to deprive their children of education, their mothers of dignity in domestic labor, their fathers the dignity of being called "sir" and not "boy" at the age of 60. Bobby did not want the responsibility of bearing witness to their pain and their rage. Witness often exposes the unspoken claims of whiteness—its privilege to hide, its ability to deflect black suffering into comparatively sterile discussions of policy that take the heat off of "me" and put it on "that."

Another conversation between a liberal white politician and five black activists went viral in 2015 when presidential candidate Hillary Clinton and members of BLM had a dramatic encounter. Clinton was compelled to forcibly reckon with the existential witness of black trauma even as she spoke of the need for sensible and substantive public policy.

* * *

On August 11, 2015, a group of activists were barred from a Clinton campaign event that focused on drug abuse, and Clinton agreed to meet with them afterward. Her interaction with Julius Jones, the 35-year-old founder of a BLM chapter in Worcester, Massachusetts, drew the most notice.[8]

He compared mass incarceration from the drug war to a "prison plantation system," adding that "until someone takes that message and speaks that truth to white people in this country so that we can actually take on anti-Blackness as a founding problem in this country, I don't believe that there is going to be a solution." With skepticism, he asked Clinton: "What in your heart has changed that's going to change the direction of this country?" It may as well have been Baldwin confronting Bobby all over again. Clinton refused to characterize her heart. "I don't believe you can change hearts," she said. "I believe you change laws. You change allocation of resources. You change the way systems operate." If all that transpired under

her potential presidency, or anyone else's administration, was a change of heart, and not the systemic
change she prescribed, "we'll be back here in 10 years
having the same conversation." Jones responded: "Respectfully . . . you don't tell black people what we need
to know, and we won't tell you all what you need to do."
Clinton fired back: "Well, *respectfully,* if that is your
position, then I will talk only to white people about
how we are going to deal with . . . very real problems."
Here was the white liberal forced to reckon with her
own behavior.

Clinton told me that she was concerned that the
"grassroots energy" of the BLM activists would not
result in actual change. "I am running for office because I believe politics really matters," she said back
then. "And it matters because we've got to harness the
energy of people, organize them, politicize them, to
bring about changes from the local level to the national
level." She mentioned the passage of the Voting Rights
Act in 1965, which she called a landmark in American history. "But [it] didn't mean that people's hearts
changed. It meant that we had the power of the law, we
had the Constitution on our side. And that was a powerful tool to change circumstances that open doors
to many people." The appeal of policy over witness is
reflected in Clinton's vocabulary and worldview. Earlier generations of blacks have also separated the body
and soul in a division of political and moral labor. The

law has been left to politicians and jurists, the heart
ceded to the clergy. The BLM activists insist on the
unity of politics and morality: The racist act is connected to the racist intent; the murdering hand is connected to the murderous heart.

Race is like religion: It has its conservative literal-
ists and fundamentalist adherents; it has liberal inter-
preters who advocate separation of church and state;
and it has radical revisionists who abandon dogma
but dote on the moral heart of the faith. Clinton, like
King and Kennedy, is a racial liberal. She seeks to
uphold the virtue of legislation and policy. BLM are
radical revisionists who embrace the intent more than
the form. They see the existential blight and bilious re-
vulsion of blackness as it courses through the veins of
this culture. This perspective has been criticized, not
just by Hillary Clinton, but by the black old guard she
wronged in her 2008 campaign who share her belief
in *getting things done*.

The rejoinder to this view, of course, is one with
which Clinton and the rest of us will eventually have
to contend. The solutions proffered in the name of
progressive racial faith—change in law, change in
policy—have no answer for the hate that trumps law,
the bigotry that adapts to whatever law is on the books
and finds a way to twist it to its advantage. Whether
any politician can truly address this conundrum is another matter.

BLM grew out of the desperate need to acknowledge the unarmed black people who were victims of violence, especially those who were being unjustly cut down in the streets by cops and racist vigilantes. BLM erupted as a hashtag when the refusal to recognize the worth and value of black life after the acquittal of George Zimmerman in the killing of Trayvon Martin led to an insistence by its three black female founders—Patrisse Cullors, Opal Tometi, and Alicia Garza—that #BlackLivesMatter. But it was from the beginning much more; it was a summons to action and quickly grew into a national movement that addressed the root causes of black suffering.

There was predictable backlash against BLM as a "racist and terrorist organization" by alt-right reactionaries and racists. Furthermore, there was little sympathy for the insistent cries for freedom and justice that were adopted by the BLM youth who mobilized for social justice. That response stands in sharp contrast to the support white protesters often garner. For example, when the students at the mostly white Marjory Stoneman Douglas High School in Parkland, Florida, mobilized for stricter gun control laws (against the vocal opposition of the NRA) in the aftermath of the killing of 17 people by a deranged gunman who was a former student there, with some small exception, they were widely greeted as heroes and supported by huge amounts of money from celebrities like George

Clooney and Oprah Winfrey. By contrast, the young folk of color who organized after countless acts of domestic racial terror carried out by law enforcement officials were roundly condemned and broadly resisted and were offered little cultural or political credence. It is clear that witness is racialized, and black witness, as it was in slavery, is never seen as legitimate. Black witness is always perceived as unjustified rage. Blackness has no victims in white eyes and therefore has no right to bear witness to whiteness at all. Bearing witness to racial injustice is always perceived as a direct threat to white supremacy and is therefore an act of hostility that must be neutralized. One of BLM's greatest contributions is to bear witness to the trauma black folk endure but that is often rendered invisible.

But BLM was prodded to move beyond that witness to embrace the nuts and bolts of sophisticated policy. On August 1, 2016, the Movement for Black Lives (M4BL), a coalition of more than 60 organizations connected with BLM, unveiled an ambitious plan, *A Vision for Black Lives: Policy Demands for Black Power, Freedom & Justice,* that demanded the channeling of resources from prison and the military to education, health, and safety; forging a democratic and just economy; and garnering black political power in an inclusive democratic framework. Historian Robin D. G. Kelley called it "a remarkable blueprint for social transformation that ought to be read and discussed by everyone."[9] BLM understands the link between heart and system, between policy and witness. Still, their insistence on giving profound weight to existential testimony and emotional self-care courts suspicion in some white, and black, political circles. And they would not let up on Clinton and other political figures, cajoling them to address the issues BLM held dear and insisting that the virtues and strengths of witness be acknowledged.

* * *

The lengths to which BLM was willing to go to challenge political figures was displayed at a campaign rally held for Clinton at Clark Atlanta University in late October 2015. There, surrounded by a younger contingent of black leaders—former Atlanta mayor Kasim Reed, former NBA player Grant Hill, R&B artists Usher and Monica—as well as civil rights legends Andrew Young, C. T. Vivian, and Congressman John Lewis, who introduced her, Clinton was greeted with great enthusiasm.

"I know that there are differences in the world we live in today," Clinton said, "and in the challenges we face, but the leaders of the civil rights movement had it right: organizing, mobilizing, and politicizing, using nonviolence, using the power of the feelings that come forward—" As if on cue, nine young BLM activists

made their way into the gymnasium, clapping, singing, and chanting "Black lives matter."

"And yes, they do," Clinton agreed. "Yes, they do.
Yes, they do, and I'm going to talk a lot about that in
a minute." The activists continued their clamor, but
Clinton was undaunted.

As the activists protested, Clinton preached, offering a remarkable run of ideas that revealed her ma-
turing grasp of the mandate the activists proffered:

> To all the young people here today, those who
> are listening, and those who are singing, let me
> say this: We need you. We need the promise of
> a rising generation of activists and organizers
> who are fearless in your advocacy and deter-
> mination. Actually, a few weeks ago, I sat down
> with some of the people here . . . [A]s I told them
> then, we have to come together as a nation to
> make the changes that they are calling for. You
> know, in that meeting a young woman said they
> spoke about being outsiders in their own coun-
> try, and those words broke my heart, coming
> from someone so young. And they also should
> stiffen our spines, because life does matter and
> we need to act like it matters.

Clinton's rhetoric, powerful as it was, failed to quell
the protesters' voices. Mayor Reed and Congressman

Lewis ranged through the crowd, attempting to calm the verbal storm. But they were finally forced to give up, and they returned to join Clinton onstage, symbolic sentinels of the black political elite. Clinton was getting her first full blast of the public agitation that BLM activists could marshal. They would not be placated: Unlike the old guard, BLM had no history with Clinton. They felt they owed her nothing.

This contrasting response to Clinton underscores a bigger black battle: one between advocates of respectability politics who believe that black decency carries its own moral force and may convince white America to treat black Americans humanely, and advocates of what may be termed *subversive* indifference—those who strategically ignore the reasons and passions of white America in calculating the merit of political response to black suffering. To be sure, there are many black folk who spurn respectability politics but who nonetheless tout an etiquette of political respect— preserve the humanity of one's opponent, listen to the other side—as necessary for social change.

But the differences between respectability politics and the etiquette of respect are blurred in the minds of those who, like BLM, practice subversive indifference. The advocates of respectability politics care about how someone like Clinton feels about them; advocates of the etiquette of respect don't seek Clinton's approval, or the approval of the black elite, as much as they seek to engage Clinton and white America in a good-faith dialogue about race on the road to transformation. BLM doesn't care for either: they neither seek the approval of Clinton—or for that matter, John Lewis or Kasim Reed—nor are they content merely to speak with the white or black powers that be. To paraphrase Marx, BLM believes that leaders and thinkers have *interpreted* the world, but the point is to *change* it. If that means practicing *politicus interruptus,* then so be it—if the result is not another conference, white paper, commission, rally, or speech, but substantive, measurable change.

I am an advocate of the etiquette of respect—primarily because I want to be heard even as I listen to others in the attempt to forge change. Those who confuse the etiquette of respect for bloodless civility mistake political kindness for weakness. It is critical to listen, even if one greatly disagrees, not only to plot further strategy and determine if what one argues is effective, but, equally important, to embody the values one seeks to impart. If the point of interrupting speech is to change behavior—a noble goal for certain—what is to keep others from practicing the same methods on those who interrupt, of interrupting the interrupters, of disrupting the disrupters? As a method of gaining audience, the politics of disruption may be invaluable; as a tool to supply the content of social change, not so much. The two, however, need not be in fatal tension. But for that to occur, there must be a concession to the back-and-forth that sometimes demands the interruption of business as usual—which often buries moral claims and political priorities beneath an avalanche of rhetoric about respect and the common good. Such rhetoric often makes the vulnerable even more invisible and keeps them from truly being heard. Instead, we should embrace the need to listen, engage, determine the efficacy of approach and method, be self-critical about what works and what doesn't, and then proceed along the path of genuine social change.

Of course, not everyone in the old guard opposes the BLM methods. Frederick Haynes, the 58-year-old orator and Dallas megachurch pastor and social activist, sees disruption as a critical method of social resistance that unites, rather than divides, multiple generations of black activists. "Nothing in this country that has progressed has happened without the politics of disruption," Haynes told me. "You can go to the Boston Tea Party: that's the politics of disruption. The ending of slavery was through the politics of disruption. Harriet Beecher Stowe's *Uncle Tom's Cabin*—that disrupted the psyche of a country that called itself a democracy. I say let's keep doing it, and let's hit the Republicans as well, because we do not progress as a people unless we disrupt what is."

Not all activist ministers agree with BLM's methods. At a black community forum on policing with

Los Angeles mayor Eric Garcetti held at LA's Hol-
man United Methodist Church, BLM disrupted the
meeting, leading pastor Kelvin Sauls to decry their
methods. "There were about 800 people here," Sauls
told the *Los Angeles Times,* "and about 750 of those
individuals were silenced because of the disrespect
that they have brought to the sanctuary as well as to
us as a congregation, misusing our hospitality."[10] It
remains to be seen whether, in the long run, this sort
of direct action at public events will be effective. But
there is no denying this point: The palpable discom-
fort that demonstrations produce forces our political
figures to grapple with new ideas. This is a productive tension.

Clinton's message seemed tailor-made for BLM
activists concerned about white privilege, institutional power, personal culpability, and political pre-
scriptions for substantive change. Some Clinton
supporters, like John Lewis, while acknowledging the
need for young activists to make "good trouble," also
said they "have to respect the right of everybody to be
heard. And you do that in a nonviolent, orderly fashion." The BLM activists, however, believed that without their actions, Clinton may never have addressed
the issues they cared about. "Disruption is a tactic that
will be here for the long run because a lot of times
conversations do not happen without pressure," Avery
Jackson, then a 20-year-old Morehouse College student, and one of the protesters, told me. "People want

a president of the United States who is going to address this, and if they want us to be quiet, they're going to have to make some change."

Julius Jones, who had spoken with Clinton in New Hampshire, agreed, characterizing these protests as a valid, and considered, tactic. "Some folks wanted us to yell at [Clinton in New Hampshire]. And some folks wanted us to talk to her," he told me. "Yes, yes, there's a difference between rejecting the politics of respectability and just a respectful conversation. And it's really important. But I also feel like the way that you get access, the reason why we were able to have a conversation with Hillary Clinton, is directly because of the actions in Seattle [when 2016 presidential candidate Senator Sanders was shut down by BLM]."

What Jones was talking about represents the crux of the conflict between the older and younger black generations. One group seeks a seat at the table—seeks power, respects the niceties of politics, values negotiation over confrontation—and the other believes the time has long since come to update King's conception of direct action with something even more compelling: immediate action. The latter may read as unrealistic to the former, and perhaps at times, even to me—after all, if we don't listen to what Clinton says after we interrupt her, there is no way to determine if she got the message. "I think you disrupt and then let her talk," Haynes said. "I don't think it's a matter of 'Just let her talk.' I daresay that much of what has been said about Black Lives Matter is on the agenda now because of the politics of disruption."

Clinton had told me that she believes that both direct activism and legislative work will be needed to enact change for black folk in this country, a fact she thought the BLM activists were starting to understand. She told me about her encounter with Brittany Packnett, a BLM activist who was on President Obama's Task Force on 21st Century Policing. When Clinton complimented Packnett in 2015 on the work she had done—calling for a National Crime and Justice Task Force and for police departments to collect better data about the race of those they stopped and arrested—and asked when the suggestions would be implemented, Packnett told Clinton the commission would expire at the end of that year.

According to Clinton, she said, "Well, you gotta get in there and say, 'No, you're not going to expire. You're going to be there.' So it's a constant: What is it we have to do? Not just to keep the issue alive, not just to have a charismatic young voice in the mix, but [to ask] how do we do the hard, boring work of building the coalitions and writing the legislation, getting reforms done across the board from the local level to the national level?" In short, how to combine policy and witness, the existential and the institutional.

* * *

Of course, any successful progressive politician, if they expect to garner the support of black folk, must find a way to speak to both the old generation and the new. And they will need to figure out how to get the heart-system and witness-policy dyad right. One way to do that has been for politicians and other activists to push BLM to find a broader framework for their concerns than just policing. BLM's remarkable *Vision* document is the fruit of such constructive pressure. "I think that's the right direction," Clinton said, even before the document appeared. "You don't want to get so broad that you lose focus, but you gotta put what you're really focused on within a broader context."

But while Clinton was happy to tell me that BLM was making progress, it is unclear whether the feeling was mutual. The BLM activists protested Clinton at Clark for nearly 30 minutes, and for nearly 30 minutes Clinton sought to speak over them.[11] The pro-Clinton crowd grew increasingly irritated and offered chants of their own like "let her talk," until security guards escorted the nine young people from the gym. "I appreciate the mayor and the congressman having my back," Clinton said, chuckling, as the crowd roared its approval. She then offered details from her criminal justice platform. She called for more responsible policing, saying "the names of young African-American men and women cut down too young is a rebuke to us all," and for an end to racial profiling. She also argued that citizens with privilege and power had a responsibility to try to see things as others do, admitting that white Americans had "close[d] our eyes to the truth," believing that "bigotry is largely behind us, that institutionalized racism no longer exists. But as you know so well, despite our best efforts and our highest hopes, America's long struggle with race is far from finished." So, in her way, Clinton seemed to have heard the young activists, even if they had not heard her.

Barack Obama never had to face the heat of Black Lives Matter as he ran for office. His slow action on police problems, and his reticence to confront racial crises, opened a leadership vacuum into which this movement slipped. Obama was a big disappointment to many of the black people who looked to him for leadership. With race, just as he had done with foreign policy, he led from behind. He offered lectures about failed black morality but, until late in his presidency, avoided embracing race as an issue, for fear that it would damage his ability to "get things done" with the white mainstream. Obama was, until his time in office was almost up, of little practical use to black folk. These are the same people who magnified his symbolic value while deflecting attention from his failure to adopt substantive policies to counter black unemployment and persistent intergenerational poverty. It was only near the end of his second term that he addressed a criminal justice system that has engulfed the lives of millions of his people. Obama and his fellow Democrats, unlike the BLM activists, steered safely clear of the folklore of race, deflecting attention from the strains of anti-blackness that thread through American history and shape this country's policies, perspectives, and politics.

Bill Clinton manipulated the racial passions of black folk frustrated by being denied access to the parlors of power. He offered a kind of racial parallelism that suggested—but never delivered—equality between black and white life and privileges. Obama, meanwhile, argued that what was good for America was good for black folk, when exactly the opposite is true: helping black folk helps America. Tamping down the war on drugs, which targeted black and brown folk, also spared millions of white youth hooked on methamphetamines and has created enormous empathy for white folk who confront opioid addiction. Strengthening the social safety net for our most vulnerable black and brown citizens also helped struggling white families hit hard by the recession. Obama's handsome black face and megakilowatt smile were enough to blind black folk to the stunning underperformance of his administration on race. If Bill Clinton gave black America *bad* policy and Obama gave black America *no* policy, then Hillary Clinton made the effort to offer good policy.

In a sense, Clinton emerged at what seemed like a strikingly unpropitious moment. Her strengths—the boring, the tedious, the serious attention to the small gestures that make big impacts—seemed ill-suited to the unruly temper of the times. But this perceived liability might have been her strongest recommendation to the black masses: She may have offered strict attention to policy that unapologetically played to black needs without ever feeling pressure—as Obama did—to disown, to begrudge the style of, explicit black advance.

Clinton said that if she won there were a host of policies her administration would put forth to help black folk: She spoke of redirecting federal resources to local and state law enforcement. She spoke to me about black unemployment, a subject Obama hardly acknowledged, the school-to-prison pipeline, which, she said, "often starts because black kids get suspended and expelled at a much higher rate." She talked about creating "real alternatives to incarceration," adding that "we don't want [black people] being put into the prison system for nonviolent, low-level offenses, but we also don't want them just thrown out on the streets. There's got to be a much better array of services that is available for people to try to get their own lives on the right track." She touted community empowerment and "the use of the federal dollar to try to support small businesses, which are still the backbone of most African-American communities"; she advocated for job training programs, addiction services, mental health treatment: the meat, the substance.

Bill Clinton and Barack Obama both made hay over their spiritual connections to Martin Luther King—but it was primarily the King who spun his dreams in public, not the King who hung his heartbreak across increasingly radical rhetoric near the end of his life—in part because King learned from Malcolm X and Stokely Carmichael the political value of black self-love and the need for black power. It was a synthesis of heart and system, of witness and policy. If our progressive politicians continue to learn from BLM, and teach them a thing or two in turn, it may not be a match made in heaven—after all, that's what many said about the relationship between liberal voters and the Obama presidency—but it may be a partnership that yields more action on race than we have had in quite some time, especially if they focus on the realities that King died fighting: structural inequality, economic desperation, racial injustice. In that way Robert Kennedy's desire for targeted public policy and the black yen for witness and prophecy might find mutual and satisfying support.

* * *

If BLM activists found Hillary Clinton wanting, another group of black thinkers and activists took their ideological beef with Clinton to an absurd length by discouraging black folk to vote—and in drawing ill-conceived and preposterous parallels between Clinton and Donald Trump. These gestures not only undercut rational black politics, but they violated the spirit of Baldwin's notion of witness and distorted the black freedom struggle's commitment to black power.

There were many reasons for Hillary Clinton's loss to Donald Trump in the 2016 election: the lack of enthusiasm among Democratic voters for Hillary Clinton, including women and African Americans; a failure of the Clinton campaign to mobilize black voters through media buys; diminished black voter registration; ongoing Republican black voter suppression tactics; purged voter rolls and polling place abnormalities and dysfunction that compromised ballots in battleground states with lots of black voters; possible Russian interference; the appeal of Donald Trump to disaffected white voters who felt that the spoils of the previous eight years had gone to black folk—a view, by the way, without a blush of empirical evidence—and a toxic backlash to the first black president in the nation's history, whose election infuriated millions of whites.

Black voting during the 2016 election took a precipitous dip.[12] In 2012, black folk were 7.6 percent of the 222,474,111 eligible American voters. In 2016, black folk were only 6.5 percent of 231,556,622 eligible voters. In 2016, black voter turnout declined significantly and fell nationally by 4.7 percentage points. In non-battleground states, black voter turnout declined by 4.3 percentage points from 2012. But in states where the election was determined by a margin of less than 10 points, black voter turnout fell by a dramatic 5.3 percentage points.[13] Black voters didn't cost Clinton the election—suppression efforts were key, and so was the spike in the white working class vote—but their dramatic decline in turnout impacted the race profoundly. The results weren't abstract or theoretical: black voter turnout slumped, the white working class flocked to the polls in droves, and Donald Trump won the White House in one of the most improbable presidential victories in history. Black activists and thinkers on the left didn't determine the election outcome, but they fed black voter skepticism that had a negative impact on black interests.

To be sure, there is longstanding black voter frustration with our problematic political situation: the Republican Party has long ignored the interests of black people, while the Democratic Party has largely taken the black vote for granted. That was even the case more than half a century ago at the Kennedy-Baldwin meeting, where Bobby warned against alienating con-servative white southern voters from the Democratic Party with too flagrant a flexing of black political muscle—which was virtually nonexistent in 1963—and too great a focus on black issues. The same preoccupa-tion with the needs of the white voter prevails today.

The belief that the Democratic Party relentlessly exploits black support while neglecting black interests is compelling and legitimate. The enormous frustra-tion is quite understandable. However, the argument that black folk shouldn't vote because of those frus-trations is hugely problematic. It is understandable that some BLM activists, and other black millennials, were turned off to the electoral process. They were disillusioned with Clinton because she had sided with her husband, President Bill Clinton, in passing welfare reform, which hurt millions of poor blacks. She agreed with him that longer, harsher sentences were needed to combat the plague of the crack epi-demic from the mid-eighties to the early nineties, prompting him to sign a draconian crime bill—with the support of many black leaders, too, and the vote of Senator Bernie Sanders, Clinton's opponent in the 2016 Democratic primaries. That bill led to the present over-incarceration of black and brown folk. Hillary also echoed social scientist John DiIulio in terming as superpredators mostly young black teen criminals who were impulsive and remorseless. DiIulio has long since repented of inventing the term, and Clinton's use of it resurfaced during her presidential run, for which she rightly was held to account.

But that wasn't all: Hillary's questionable history pegged her as racially radioactive. This included the infamous "3 a.m. phone call" commercial in the 2008 campaign that suggested, in racial code, that Obama was unreliable as a black man to answer the call of duty, spooking the nation's white hinterland; her argument that "Obama's support among working, hardworking Americans, *white* Americans is weakening again"; her claim that whites "who had not completed college were supporting me"[14]; and her argument that Martin Luther King's "dream began to be realized only when President Johnson signed the Civil Rights Act," seeming to discredit King's efforts.[15] By the 2016 campaign, however, Clinton had developed far more progressive views on race. And her opponent was a likely bigot, or at least a man who is quite friendly with racist forces that spew venom at black folk. But neither of those things kept young activists and voters from viewing Clinton with great skepticism.

Neither did it keep activist and intellectual Michelle Alexander, the renowned author of *The New Jim Crow,* from hammering Clinton in an essay in *The Nation,* claiming that Hillary didn't deserve the black vote because of her support for the crime bill and welfare reform. (Alexander was curiously silent about Obama's refusal to target public policy to aid black folk in his eight years in office.) Alexander wrote that Clinton "believes that she can win this game in 2016 because this time she's got us, the black vote, in her black pocket—her lucky card," and Alexander felt people should refuse to play her game and realize that it's time "to reshuffle this deck."[16] Nor did the prospect of Trump dissuade Cornel West from assailing Clinton as the "Milli Vanilli of American politics," offering "lip service" to progressive ideas but "when it comes to policy," supporting the crime bill and yanking "the rug from under welfare."[17] It is important to remember that Clinton held no office when she made the claims about crime or the need for welfare reform.

Many young activists and voters embraced Alexander's and West's views; they were understandably tired of voting for what they thought of as the lesser of two evils—tired of making a choice, as one black voter put it, because she didn't like Trump, and didn't trust Clinton, "between being stabbed and being shot." Another young black woman said that Trump is "a racist, and she is a liar, so really what's the difference in choosing both or choosing neither?" They followed in the footsteps of renowned scholar and activist W.E.B. Du Bois, who, in a 1956 essay in *The Nation,* "Why I Won't Vote," declared that "I shall not go to the polls. I have not registered. I believe that democracy has so far disappeared in the United States that no 'two evils' exist. There is but one evil party with two names, and it will be elected despite all I can do or say."[18] This electoral fatalism was passed down to many black voters.

If not possessed of Du Bois's fatalism, some scholar activists urged black folk to practice an ill-advised selective voting. Religious studies scholar Eddie Glaude and political scientist Frederick Harris argued in *Time* magazine that black voters should become "strategic voters" as part of their "Blank-Out Campaign."[19] Black voters in red states should "vote as they usually do for the candidates, down the ballot," while leaving their choice for the president blank, or cast a ballot for a third-party candidate. As pressure voters, they would "put their presidential votes to better use than as wasted votes for the Democratic Party," which had little chance of winning in those states. They cited Alabama as an example. Black voters contributed roughly 70 percent of Obama's share of the vote in Alabama in both his presidential runs in 2008 and 2012. But those votes were "inconsequential" because they couldn't keep the state's nine electoral votes from going to John McCain in 2008 and Mitt Romney in 2012, both of whom bested Obama with 60 percent of the vote. Glaude and Harris argued that by "converting 'wasted' presidential votes into 'none of the above' or support for third-party candidates in Oklahoma, Arizona and other deep red states in the South—the

Confederacy, essentially—black voters would exert pressure on party leaders to not take black voters and their issues for granted."

Glaude and Harris seemed to make a compelling case for strategic voting by black voters in red states, except that black folk beyond the red states also seemed to follow their advice. Moreover, the flaw of such an approach was revealed in the 2017 special election to fill the seat vacated by Alabama senator Jeff Sessions, who became attorney general in 2017. Although it was not a presidential race, it was nonetheless a high-profile contest—in part because of the presence of accused child predator Roy Moore as the Republican nominee—that seemed very unlikely to put Democratic candidate Doug Jones in Congress since Alabama hadn't sent a Democrat to the Senate since 1992. And yet, aided by the scandal dogging Moore, and an intense get-out-the-vote effort that netted a rich bounty of black voters, especially black women, Jones garnered a stunning victory. Had black voters practiced Glaude's and Harris' strategic voting, they would have lost the opportunity to help elect a Democrat to the Senate under a Trump presidency—in a state Trump won easily—and would not be witness to the appointment of the only black chief of staff for a Democratic senator. (Republican senators Tim Scott of South Carolina—who is black—and Jerry Moran of Kansas, have black chiefs of staff.)

Similarly, in Mississippi in 2014, Republican senator Thad Cochran won a hotly contested race when black citizens voted for him to keep an arch-conservative opponent, Chris McDaniel, from replacing Cochran in the Senate. Because Mississippi has a semi-open primary that permits any registered voter to participate in a party runoff if they have not voted in the first primary of a different party, the mobilization of historically Democratic black voters who had not voted in the primary edged Cochran to victory. It is irresponsible of black activists and thinkers to encourage black people not to vote, or to vote strategically as argued in the Blank-Out Campaign. As we saw in 2016, it runs the risk of putting into office forces and figures that are hostile to the interests of black communities.

As these two instances show, black voters are savvy enough to understand that ideological purity is an enemy to effective politics. Commitment to a politics that privileges ideological preferences over the good of the masses of blacks is the ultimate subversion of black political power. It is also the ultimate betrayal of the spirit of Baldwin and his compatriots in that room—all of whom understood that it was Jerome Smith, more than they, who stood for the interests of the black masses. And his primary effort was to win black suffrage for the masses.

It is intriguing that black leftists, who often make analyses of the material conditions of people or institutions to account for their position or status, rarely apply the same metric to themselves. Many of them are well-heeled academics or professionals whose economic interests will not suffer, and may even be enhanced, by a Republican administration that offers tax cuts to wealthier Americans. It is even more irresponsible for black activists and thinkers to argue that there was little difference between Hillary Clinton and Donald Trump; that, as Cornel West put it, Trump was "a neo-fascist catastrophe" and Clinton was "a neo-liberal disaster." Such thinking helped open the door to a man whose policies and personal witness are rooted in racist thinking.

Not only has Donald Trump fostered a resurgence of white supremacy, his administration has been hostile to the interests of black folk. Attorney General Jeff Sessions—who has made explicit his belief that critical aspects of law enforcement are rightfully built on an "Anglo American" heritage and foundation—has directed the Department of Justice to "pull back" on civil rights lawsuits and investigations of police departments. That is a stunning reversal of the progress made by Attorney General Eric Holder who, under Obama, led the Justice Department in more investigations of police departments than his predecessors under Clinton and Bush combined. Leftist ideologues have, ironically, undermined justice for victims of police misconduct. Trump's nomination of Justice Neil

Gorsuch—and potentially another Supreme Court justice in the future—and his nomination of hundreds of federal judges, is reshaping the highest courts in the land and tilting them further rightward.

Under Trump, the Department of Labor has folded its Office of Federal Contract Compliance Programs into the Equal Employment Opportunity Commission (EEOC). This is a huge hindrance to the federal government's ability to monitor the abuses of contractors in a systematic fashion because the Labor Department's office is supposed to audit companies with government contracts for discrimination, while the EEOC is charged with responding to individual complaints of discrimination. The Trump administration has effectively disrupted the process, just as it has endangered the commitment to environmental justice within the Environmental Protection Agency. The list goes on.

If segments of the black left harshly criticized Clinton for her neoliberal policies, they should have far greater reason to lament the racist policies of the Trump administration. Stephen Miller, the White House senior policy advisor with close ties to right-wing media outlet Breitbart, was pivotal in drafting and rolling out Trump's vicious travel ban against select Muslim countries. A well-known white nationalist, Miller worked in communications for the nutty and bigoted former Minnesota congresswoman Michele Bachmann, and later worked for former Alabama senator Jeff Sessions, who has his own history of troubling racial comments and shares with Miller hard-line anti-immigration and anti-globalist beliefs.

Because of his writing in high school and college—including attacking Maya Angelou for "racial paranoia" and blasting a Latino student organization as a "radical national Hispanic group that believes in racial superiority"—Miller was called by *Politico* "a deeply unsettling figure, even to many in his own party." *Politico* argued that even when Miller was Trump's warm-up act on the campaign trail, there was "something eerily vintage about Miller's stump speeches" in the "combination of their substance—vilifying immigrants as killers, the promise of nativist glory days ahead—and their delivery with a calm face around a loud, droning mouth, slicked-back hair and sharp suit, floridly invoking powerful cabals against the people." His xenophobic passions and racist sentiments harken back to a black-and-white era on television and in the culture at large when immigrants and people of color "knew their places." Trump plucked Miller from the far-right political fringe and put him in place to shape policy for his presidency. When White House chief strategist Steve Bannon was fired, Miller remained behind as an acolyte of white nationalist thought offering ideological support to the ideas of white supremacist zealots.[20]

* * *

Just as Bobby Kennedy argued with Baldwin and his activist friends about politics and personal testimony, enlivening our ideas about how policy and witness fuel each other, the activist and #MeToo founder Tarana Burke is adding another dimension to the conversation. Burke is a fiercely brave and intelligent black woman who sparked a social movement by insisting on telling all the truth about black and other American lives—including the suffering of black girls and women.

"I come from a long line of a family of Pan African and black nationalists . . . I've done a lot of work around racial justice, economic justice coming up from my teenage years to my twenties," Burke tells me.

It became clear to Burke that black folk were not addressing the sexual violence that was tearing our communities apart. She had gleaned from her elders the first rule of organizing: to address people's needs—food, clothing, and shelter—before seeking to organize them. Beyond those basic needs, she saw that black communities are riddled with trauma.

> I started doing the work around #MeToo because I saw that the young people we were working with were struggling with [trauma and sexual violence], and nobody was really

speaking to it. And so it just felt like the skill I had acquired over the years as an organizer could be used in some way to start doing this work in our community around sexual violence . . . And that's the place where it really was rooted—that somebody has to represent our community in terms of this issue, because it's not just a small issue at the bottom of a checklist. It's huge and pervasive. And we have to be honest about it.

Burke understands the power of personal witness, too, in engaging the complicated issue of sexual violence in our communities that is shrouded in taboo.

When we started doing the work I used an idea called empowermental empathy, which is the idea that we are empowered by the empathy we received from another person when that empathy connects to our trauma. So if somebody is sympathetic to you, and they don't know what you've been through, they may say, "Oh, my God, I'm sorry that thing happened to you." And that'll usually put a distance between the two of you. Like, it happened to you, not me. And it's like pity. "I'm sorry for you." But when you tell me something that's the deepest, darkest secret you've held, something that's the most traumatic thing you've been through, and what I say to you is, "Yeah, that happened to me too." And it may be different, it may not be the same circumstances. But that underlying trauma that's left over is the same. And so it builds an empathetic connection between folks immediately that draws you closer, rather than putting a distance between you.

#MeToo and BLM have forced us to contend with the moral and existential dimensions of blackness in a way that has been missing in our politics for quite some time—even as both movements have embraced the need for policy as well. But the unfortunate surrender of the black left to ideological purity has lessened its use to the black masses, forgetting a lesson that Baldwin and his fellow thinkers and activists never forgot: the point of witness, and the policy that it informs, is, always, the achievement of justice for the black folk witnesses claim to speak for. Anything less than that, any idea other than that, is but a roadblock to genuine change.

THE ACTIVISTS 2

BAD NIGGERS

In March 1969, James Baldwin appeared before a House Select Subcommittee convened in New York City. He was there to testify in support of a House bill to establish a national commission on "Negro History and Culture." At one point, Baldwin, who'd brought along Malcolm X's widow, Betty Shabazz, to say a few words, suggested that black heroes weren't viewed kindly by white America.

"Yes, but you must understand that, speaking as black Americans, my heroes have always been [seen] from the point of view of white Americans as bad niggers," Baldwin said. "Cassius Clay is one of my heroes but not one of yours."

Baldwin asked that the congressmen recognize the role black heroes played in American life "and the reasons why all my heroes came to such bloody ends." Baldwin went on to say that Ali had "been hanged by the public as a bad nigger," and that he was "an example to every other Negro man. This time he called him "Muhammad Ali Clay," insisting, perhaps unconsciously, on combining his pre-conversion surname with his Muslim name. This was far different from boxer Ernie Terrell's refusal to recognize Ali's Islamic name, a sin for which Ali brutally punished Terrell in the ring, repeatedly asking him, as he mercilessly pummeled the fighter, "What's my name?" Baldwin argued that until black heroes became the heroes of white America, a bitterness would rage that would destroy the ghetto and the larger city.[1]

The next year, in an open letter to Angela Davis, Baldwin got Ali's name right and even traced the political significance of his name change. Baldwin argued that Ali was offering a different sort of opportunity than the usual emotional catharsis to be had by watching a poor black boy become a rich boxer. Ali brought an opportunity for learning about ourselves and our moral limits, about how something bigger than a payday was at stake for a prominent black athlete, something that could teach the people about courage and integrity. Baldwin wrote that "when Cassius Clay became Muhammad Ali and refused to put on that uniform (and sacrificed all that money!) a very different impact was made on the people and a very different kind of instruction had begun."

In an open letter to President Jimmy Carter in 1977, Baldwin drew attention to a distorted view of patriotism that saluted a cloth stitched by secessionists while deriding the fidelity of a man who clung nobly to his principles. "When we marched on Montgomery, the Confederate flag was flying from the dome of the Capitol: this gesture can be interpreted as *insurrection,*" Baldwin wrote. "But when Muhammad Ali decided to be *true to his faith* and refused to join the Army, the wrath of an entire Republic was visited on his head, he was stripped of his title, and was not allowed to work. In short, his countrymen decided to break him, and it is not their virtue that they failed. It is *his* virtue." Ironically, Baldwin notes, a Muslim believer evinced more virtue than the Christian democracy that tested him.

The heroism that Ali embodied is in line with the heroism evoked by Jerome Smith in the meeting with Kennedy. It was to their credit that all the celebrities who gathered recognized Smith's superior sacrifice. Yet most of them were at the meeting because of their willingness to lay their fame on the line in defense of their brothers and sisters who couldn't be heard the same way, in the same places, in a way that might make a big difference. A special burden fell on the shoulders of those who had been blessed with great talent: they must use their station to tell the truth; to, in Baldwin's words, be "a witness." If that was true in 1963, it remains true today.

There can be no denying that, for many white Americans, our heroes are now their heroes—well, at least our champions are theirs; black and white folk both love Michael Jordan and, to a large degree, LeBron James. But James' elevated stature is compromised for some because, through his shrewd use of free agency, he nearly singlehandedly changed the terms of players leaving or joining a team. For others that made him a hero. He has also been outspoken on race and social issues, even sharply criticizing President Trump, putting him occasionally at odds with conservative white America and one of their loudest outlets, Fox News.

In fact, a Fox host, Laura Ingraham, shot back at James and fellow superstar Kevin Durant, both of whom had expressed contrary views about Trump, telling them to "shut up and dribble."[2] Many interpreted that as a racist wolf whistle to "keep your black mouth shut and entertain us."

James called on the earlier examples of Ali, Jim Brown, Bill Russell, and Jackie Robinson to suggest his membership in a distinguished tradition of black athletes who have spoken up for the black masses. "I will not just shut up and dribble," he said. "So, thank you, whatever her name is . . . I get to sit up here and talk about what's really important and how I can help change kids. It lets me know that everything I've been saying is correct for her to have that type of reaction. But we will definitely not shut up and dribble. I will definitely not do that. I mean too much to society, I mean too much to the youth, I mean too much to so many kids that feel like they don't have a way out and they need someone to help lead them out of the situation they're in."

Former professional quarterback Colin Kaepernick's one-man protest against police misconduct and other flaws in the justice system led him to take a knee during the playing of the national anthem. He was portrayed as an un-American traitor to American values and was nearly unanimously detested by the white front offices of NFL teams across the league. Kaepernick found himself out of a job after declaring free agency despite being better than half the league's starting quarterbacks. President Trump eventually referred to the mostly black players who mirrored Kaepernick in silent forms of protest as "sons of bitches."[3]

Contemporary athletes face some of the same problems that earlier generations of athletes confronted. The responsibilities of the "blessed Negro," the duties of the gifted black, reside, in part, in saying what his less-well-off, less-well-connected, or less-well-listened-to brothers and sisters might say or do if they were in his spot, or skin, or had his voice or platform.

* * *

"You that nigga that can talk," the famous voice softly ribbed me in an airport terminal in 1993. It was Muhammad Ali, the towering, though visibly shaking, former heavyweight champion of the world. His mischievous eyes still glowed with the wonder of life. Ali's vernacular compliment was far truer of his life than mine. In his golden days he talked relentlessly, courageously, even dangerously, about black folk and racial injustice in America. And, of course, about how great and pretty he was.

Ali's boasting was a proxy for group assertion at a time when such a thing was wildly unpopular. His words echoed the desire for black folk to be confident in their self-worth. Black men were especially drawn to Ali and wanted to be just as unapologetic as the champ in voicing black pride. When he rhymed we rhymed too, believing that we could spit homespun verse to proclaim our majesty. We too could "float like a butterfly and sting like a bee." We too could "rumble, young man, rumble." We too could say that we "shook up the world."

I met Muhammad Ali for the first time a year before our airport encounter. I had been invited to participate in a 1992 symposium on his life at Miami

University of Ohio, which featured talks by eight thinkers and scribes, including renowned sportswriter and Ali biographer Robert Lipsyte. I was still a graduate student at Princeton and just grateful to be in the room with the champ to parse Ali's complicated legacy in several no-holds-barred sessions. In my talk I imagined him as a poetic forerunner to hip hop. It made sense to me that Ali's daughter Maryum "May May" Ali was a rapper who sampled and transformed her father's prose and poetry.

Ali's outpouring of words outside the ring marked him as a man to be heard and seen. In the early twentieth century, heavyweight champ Jack Johnson's despised dark skin forced him to pay a steep professional and cultural price for beating up white men and winning their women too. Near mid-century, the fists of heavyweight champ Joe Louis spoke when he dropped German boxer Max Schmeling and struck a blow for American democracy and black pride. Ali didn't at first seem to fit their mold; the self-proclaimed "Louisville Lip" came off as little more than a cocky contender. It was soon clear that Ali's verses were a mash-up of literature and theory—Paul Laurence Dunbar meets Noam Chomsky. Ali twisted language to suit his pugilistic purposes and transformed the political grammar of black identity. The surface structure of Ali's brashness pointed to the deeper structure of his quest for black self-respect, and ours too.

Hip hop great Jay-Z captured this idea when he said that "Muhammad Ali is one of my heroes because when he was saying, 'I'm pretty,' he was saying that to all of us, he made all of us feel like we were pretty. 'I'm pretty, I'm a bad man, I'm pretty.' You gotta figure this was a time when we were considered ugly, so he wasn't saying that as a boast to walk inside the ring, he was saying that as a boast for all of us."

For most of our history black folk were viewed as ugly creatures who lacked European charm and beauty. Black folk were considered biologically ugly too. We were the genetic junk of a race that drew from the genes and chromosomes of an impure species. Black folk were morally ugly, soulless savages seeking to satisfy appetites without higher purpose. And black folk were seen as mentally ugly too— intellectually inferior beings incapable of divining life's deeper meanings. Ali, like the best rappers, was, as best he could, speaking back to all that. To be sure, it wasn't in the scholarly fashion of W.E.B. Du Bois, though it should be remembered that Du Bois' hope that scientific proof of black humanity could uproot racial tyranny was dashed by the realization that bigotry never bows to reason.

Ali blazed the path for hip hop artists placing vernacular speech in the service of truth, though such speech is always at first seen as a mockery of taste and pedigree. That's true whether the art in question is the sorrow song of the slave plantation, the blues of the urban enclave, or the rap of the concrete jungle. Such views didn't just come from black cultural outsiders; they sprang from native speakers as well. Reading and writing for enslaved blacks was a matter of life and death, a fact that has often compelled black elites and others to favor highbrow instead of gutbucket literacy. Ali, like the rappers who came behind him, fought racial denigration outside black culture and faced class disdain from within.

The truths he told were raw and blunt; for instance, that black folk hated our broad noses and big lips. But Ali knew those noses were made to whiff the sweet scent of self-love, and those lips, yes, those lovely lips, which contained a world large enough to swim in, were meant to proclaim our beauty and greatness. The magic and charm of Ali's incantatory street doggerel is the divine way it showed that we were the gods of our self-making and our bold self-loving.

Ali's speech could not be separated from his spirit, his tongue from his temple of worship. When Ali announced to the world that he would no longer answer to his slave name of Cassius Marcellus Clay— a name that rolled off the tongue in near alliterative euphony—but that he would instead adopt a name bestowed on him by the leader of a black religion, he certainly "shook up the world," as he had when he battered heavyweight champion Sonny Liston to the canvas. Ali stood in for every black person who has had their sanity questioned for refusing to pray the way they were taught to pray by those whose gods and rituals were meant to undo us by containing and deflating us. Ali "whupped" Liston—a victory he forecast in homespun verse spat at the "baddest man on the planet," the unofficial title that the heavyweight champ, whoever he was, used to hold until at least Mike Tyson. Ali also pummeled the racist beliefs that had created Liston's hardscrabble childhood and painful adulthood—and that of every other black man who shared his tragic, difficult, impossible fate. Ali laced up his gloves against a white world that seemed undefeatable and proved its vulnerability one blow at a time.

That fight wasn't always perfect, of course, especially when Ali sucker-punched an opponent with the very ideas he meant to defeat. Like many black men who surrender to the temptation to become oppressor for a day, or for several of them, Ali occasionally did the white man's work for him, as when he viciously painted Joe Frazier as a racial sellout during the buildup to their third and most consequential epic battle. Ali taunted Frazier before their final fight for the heavyweight championship in the Philippines in 1975 with his most derisive rhymes ever, proclaiming on national television, as he playfully pummeled a toy primate, "It's going to be a thrilla in Manila when I kill that gorilla."[4] Ali was a 6'3" light-skinned black man in a world that agreed with his self-proclaimed handsomeness. Frazier was a 5'11" dark-skinned black man who was widely viewed as anything but pretty. Ali's heartless attack on Frazier couldn't be merely seen as his usual attempt to get inside his opponent's head. The racial enemy that Ali had so brilliantly resisted, even truculently disputed, remained inside his mind; and in his psychic bloodstream flowed color-specific stereotypes that temporarily suppressed his immunity to black self-hate. Ali projected onto Frazier's chocolate body the nation's sacramental disdain for darkness that is religiously transmitted in its catechism of colorism. That so many black men remain color-struck in who we love and dislike suggests that Ali's bitter ignorance 40 years ago still burns in our brains and bodies.

Although we didn't speak of his ugly offense to Frazier at the symposium, Ali did admit error in dealing with Malcolm X. "I was wrong about him," Ali gently confessed to me about the man largely responsible for inspiring his conversion to Islam. After Malcolm fell out of favor with the Nation of Islam's leader, the Honorable Elijah Muhammad, a chorus of voices within the religious group dubbed Malcolm a traitor and left him vulnerable to some members' murderous rage. Ali turned his back on Malcolm too, a decision he later regretted. It is sad that black men sometimes can't disagree without fatal consequences, whether in the streets or in more polite circles, where we thrash each other with unkind words that separate us from former friends. Malcolm died before Ali could seek his forgiveness.

While Ali didn't reconcile with Malcolm, white society managed to reconcile with the former champ. Ali had exulted in unpardonable blackness by embracing a black God and displaying unquenchable loyalty to black folk by loving his people unceasingly and without apology. He developed a grassroots manner to measure white offense against blackness. He produced a demonology that drew from the Nation of Islam and the black power struggles that he both inspired and absorbed. Ali reveled in valiant blackness, a courageous moral and philosophical argument that black life be treated with dignity and respect. He presaged our contemporary Black Lives Matter practice of both naming and resisting black animus while linking such gestures to practical politics. His was surely an intuitional rebellion, a matter of criticizing what he in his gut knew to be wrong, but his actions were also connected to broader freedom struggles in black America and throughout the black diaspora, where he was madly loved.

Ali made war on war. He held out as a conscientious objector against the bloodbath in Vietnam. He offered black folk and other allies a lesson about how to link local and global forms of oppression in one turn of phrase. Even if it's a misquote, it manages to capture Ali's true intention: "Ain't No Vietcong ever called me [a] nigger."[5] In truth Ali said that his conscience "won't let me go shoot my brother, or some darker people, or some poor hungry people in the mud for big powerful America. And shoot them for what? *They never called me nigger,* they never lynched me, they didn't put no dogs on me, they didn't rob me of my nationality, rape and kill my mother and father . . . Shoot them for what? Just take me to jail."[6]

Ali was even more forceful about the link between domestic and international racial terror, and colonialism and oppression, when he declared that "I'm not gonna help nobody get something my Negroes don't have. If I'm gonna die, I'll die now right here fighting you, if I'm gonna die. You my enemy. My enemies are white people, not Viet Congs or Chinese or Japanese. You my opposer when I want freedom. You my opposer when I want justice. You my opposer when I want equality. You won't even stand up for me in America for my religious beliefs, and you want me to go somewhere and fight, but won't even stand up for me here at home."[7]

It is not that Ali "matured" and gave up his ferocious social conscience as much as America caught up to his progressive ideas—at least on the question and costs of the Vietnam War and, to a lesser degree, on the racial crises at home. The country has yet to acknowledge the link Ali drew between racial injustice at home and war abroad, where people of color are common targets of American politics or, as Malcolm X put it, "the victims of democracy."[8] Ali boldly built his views about what was happening in any number of "over there's" with a strict attention to what was happening "over here." "Here" and "there" mattered because the different geographies didn't exhaust the common ideologies that underlay their misfortunes. Ali challenged America to face up to its political hypocrisy and to acknowledge its moral shortcomings as the common points of reference in any serious discussion of war and race on both shores.

As the nation warmed up to his view of things, Ali's image changed too; he went from troublemaker to peacemaker, from rebel to saint. That change had as much to do with political and social amnesia—America often forgets what it seeks, or fails, to defeat—as it did with the admission that Ali's vision of America was more compelling, freer, truer, more capacious than the cramped, crabby, clubby vision of white racial nationalism. Like the great thinkers and leaders who preceded him—from Du Bois, to Anna Julia Cooper, to Ida B. Wells-Barnett, to Paul Robeson, to Pauli Murray, and to King and Malcolm—Ali's embrace of the world's beleaguered and downtrodden masses forced the nation to come to grips with its foul treatment of its own citizens of color. Thus, like those figures, Ali's insistence that America do the right thing was far more loyal to the nation's ideals than those figures who savaged the once-deposed champ in the name of American patriotism.

For many of his admirers Ali's transition from pariah to prophet, from scourge to icon, stands as a sharp contrast to his previous radical political activism. For them Ali's criticism of the nation seems to have given way to his embrace of America. That is far too simplistic a conclusion. The progress the nation made toward the ideals Ali fought for opened up space for him to fight injustice in a far less volatile environment. As America caught up to Ali's political vision, it pushed closer to a redemptive core: humanitarianism is not a substitute for justice, but may be one measure of its fulfillment.

This should be kept in mind as contemporary expressions of black radicalism and social resistance are often unfavorably compared to Ali's post-sixties humanitarian efforts. Such a vexing pivot depends on denying the value of Ali's earlier radicalism, and ignoring how his embrace of black love and black politics forged a path toward progressive humanitarianism. Those who profess to love Ali but despise current black protest—against police brutality, against voter suppression, against environmental racism—fundamentally misunderstand his political vision and moral sophistication.

A few prominent examples suggest how those distortions work. As long as LeBron James played basketball with a smile on his face, he was celebrated, and his charitable efforts in the community were lauded. Yet when he argued that racism played a role in the fevered responses to him leaving the Cleveland Cavaliers for the Miami Heat a few years back, he was sternly taken to task, just as he was criticized in some quarters for tweeting out a photo of his Miami Heat team donning hoodies in solidarity with the fallen black teen Trayvon Martin.

When all-pro cornerback Richard Sherman quietly played his position, he was hailed, but when he said that those calling him a "thug" because of his demonstrative on-field behavior were using it as a euphemism for the "N" word, he was lambasted. Beyoncé is embraced as a global icon of black genius when she performs, but when she spoke up about police brutality and defended the Black Lives Matter movement, former New York mayor Rudy Giuliani pounced on her, and some police departments swore not to protect her as she toured. Shedding tears over Ali's death while ignoring the tears of those who suffer today soils Ali's heroic legacy; extolling Ali's courage as a spokesman for truth while pillorying those who dare tell the truth now is a rejection of Ali too. Black protest is a form of black humanitarianism and, in fact, is its prelude and often its most righteous incarnation. The critical effort to see black folk as humane, as viable participants in humanitarian enterprise, is a political battle.

The price Ali paid for his moral courage was steep, including the sacrifice of riches and reputation, and the loss of time to be able to perfect his craft at the height of his transcendent and luminous powers. But the price to his body for his stubborn persistence in the fight game was also incalculably grave. Ali's physical courage in the face of debilitating Parkinson's disease went far beyond his athletic valor—as great as that was. His management of the disease was a metaphor for other black folk's battles, trapped inside stifling bodies of belief as they seek to negotiate their existence with a measure of grace and dignity.

Ali's suffering highlights the deep elegance and high drama of his halcyon days of performance, when black masculine style was projected in both the ring and beyond. Ali's solo performances were pitched against the canvas of cloth and history—they were ringing endorsements of black male bravado as a form of both personal self-expression and a force for racial solidarity. In the ring, Ali's fluttering force not only came down in formidable flourishes; it was also a précis of black male survival in a world against which black men matched wits and fists. That Ali literally walked, or danced, his talk, and then gave it performative zest by translating it into the political sphere, completed a circle of creation for which Ali's boxing was a powerful metaphor.

Ali performed magic tricks—making a key turn over, transforming a scarf into a wand—in defiance of the thudding literalism of the decline he suffered in his physical and motor skills, though never in his sharp and playful mind. Despite the withering diminishment of the physical gifts for which he was known, and the silencing of the tongue that once flamed with timeless truths, Ali soldiered on and held fast to his beliefs—that Islam brings peace, that blackness brings greater humanity, that protest and resistance bring greater justice. But then America has always been in love with change in reverse, in the safely settled past, not the dangerously changeable present. We prefer our heroes dead or quiet; Ali's silenced tongue surely hurried him into an iconic space that may have been impossible for him to occupy had he been able to continue to raise his voice against injustice.

Ali's magic feats were a delightful distraction for both Ali and the viewer, but his far greater magic was the relentless pursuit of good in the midst of unimaginable suffering. In that sense, he represented the greatest achievements that black people have conjured when facing odds that most might not survive. As much as he meant to the world, as much as he belonged to that world, what he meant to black people most of all can never be measured in merely physical acts alone.

While Ali's enduring contributions resonate still, it is good to reflect on other beloved athletes who have challenged injustice and protested oppression, in his day and ours.

* * *

When former San Francisco 49ers quarterback Colin Kaepernick decided to kneel during the performance of the national anthem to pay homage to black victims of police brutality, closing the gulf between patriotic ideals and the reality of black suffering, he was, predictably, pilloried. Kaepernick was met with the same charges of most every black person—whether it was Frederick Douglass or Barack Obama, Sojourner Truth or Maxine Waters, Jack Johnson or football player Malcolm Jenkins—who dared speak out against injustice: that he is un-American, unpatriotic, disrespectful, and ungrateful.

These and other charges rain down on those who challenge the nation to achieve justice for black folk. The same thing happened to the track stars John Carlos and Tommie Smith when they raised their black-gloved fists in a black-power salute at the 1968 Olympics in Mexico City to protest the injustices black people faced back home. I remember seeing that gesture, as a nine-year-old boy in Detroit. Carlos and Smith were deemed un-American and disrespectful. Brent Musburger, a sports writer at the time, called them "black-skinned storm troopers."[9] Watching Kaepernick now brings a great deal of admiration and pride in his willingness to take a stand no matter the cost to his career and reputation. It very well may be that history will vindicate his courageous stand the way it has done with Smith and Carlos, and, before them, with Muhammad Ali.

Ironically, Kaepernick has been accused of disrespecting an American flag that was long ago replaced by the Confederate flag for millions of white southerners. Those who hoist the Confederate flag indulge in romantic treason—since it is the emblem of secession from our country—often at, or on the way to, American football stadiums. He is said, too, to dishonor military veterans, though it is hard to see how, since the very freedoms for which they fought guarantee Kaepernick his dissent. Many Americans wrongly think of the military as the exclusive, or primary, guardian of American pride and patriotism. However, only in a totalitarian society does the military define, instead of defend, what it means to be American. We must never lose the battle for democracy in such careless formulations. We must not surrender to bullets and bombs what can only be had by belief and behavior—like the encouragement of dissent, the tolerance of wide disagreement about what it means to be American, and the freedom to protest for freedom.

It was no less a hero than our nation's first black Major League baseball player, Jackie Robinson, who declared that if "I had to choose tomorrow between the Baseball Hall of Fame and full citizenship for my people, I would choose full citizenship time and again."[10] Robinson's poignant words reveal the passion many black athletes have for equality. His words also remind us of the crucial role that black sports figures have played in the fight for justice. At this highly charged political moment, black athletes remain a vital force in the black quest for full emancipation. Remembering Robinson's words might dispel the myth that sports have been—or, indeed, are best seen as— divided from politics.

But there is another criticism reserved for the black athlete: that their wealth and fame mean they have little to complain about, and when they speak up, they are being ungrateful for the privileges they enjoy. Yet that is just the point—at their best, the black blessed have always spoken up for the black beleaguered.

Americans who are angry with Kaepernick often forget how black entertainers and athletes have used their fame to break down barriers of discrimination. Singer Ray Charles helped to desegregate concert halls; Jackie Robinson integrated an entire league.

Entertainers and athletes also helped to combat fear of black culture and encouraged the acceptance of black talent. They did something even more crucial that continues to this day: they convinced white America that the folk these athletes loved and admired were just as worthy of support and respect.

Many whites are upset and offended when they encounter black athletes who step out of character and break the mythology of a raceless and neutral American identity. This is especially true when it comes to protest: these athletes prove "they," the wealthy and lauded, are just like the rest of "them," the rest of "us" blacks: concerned, but more likely obsessed, with race.

There is an even greater psychological drama at play, too, that is quite tricky. If these athletes represent the cream of the black crop, it means, arguably, that they are superior to the average white person as well. But that truth is difficult for most whites to acknowledge and absorb. One of the advantages of white supremacy is that it convinces white folk that they are better than even the exceptional black person. That, however, is a curious equation: black exceptionalism hardly equals white normalcy. Such a belief is harder to sustain in an era where the exploits, excesses, and luxuries of black athletes are ubiquitous and can hardly be ignored. That may also be why there is a constant emphasis on how these rich black guys have nothing to complain about. The shift in the white mindset is clear:

black athletes have gone from representing the group to engaging in apolitical individual expression.

White folk applauding the achievements of athletes in the past—and in many cases, in the present—broke down psychological barriers to racial progress. The broader society was encouraged to at least rethink belief in the notion of black inferiority, and to question if all the stereotypes about black folk are true. In the same way that President Donald Trump is the fleshly definition of white supremacy as he draws comparisons between bigotry and those who protest it, black athletes are, and were, the ready translation of the goals and aspirations of the black masses. "You'll never know how easy you and Jackie and [Larry] Doby and Campy [Roy Campanella] made it for me to do my job by what you did on the baseball field," Martin Luther King, Jr., said to baseball superstar Don Newcombe a few weeks before King was assassinated in Memphis in 1968.[11] Newcombe was humbled. "Imagine, here is Martin getting beaten with billy clubs, bitten by dogs and thrown in jail, and he says we made his job easier."

The billy club and the baseball bat are competing weapons in the war for the mind of white America. The brutal swing of the billy club on besieged black bodies can be symbolically fought by the sweet swing of a black star at the plate. If baseball was once America's pastime, so, too, was hatred, and fear, of black people. But increasingly, in the physics of race, it became more difficult for two objects to occupy the same space at the same time: the preservation of a society that prevented black folk from rising ran headlong into an appreciation for the athletic gifts—and, by extension, the humanity—of black folk. Robinson, Doby, Campy, and Newcombe were the easiest translation of what the civil rights movement aimed for: give black folk a chance, treat us fairly, make one set of rules for us all to abide by, and we will do well. In our day, what Kaepernick and his cohort are shooting for is similar: don't assume black people are thugs, don't fear us because we are black, give us a chance to live as we explain ourselves to the police.

But symbolic representation isn't enough. It makes sense for athletes to raise their voices beyond the field of play. If they have built up cultural capital and garnered enormous success, it means that considerable quarters of white America are not only paying—they are paying attention. The money athletes make may not be as important as the mark they can leave on the minds of those who admire them. Therefore, many of them are compelled to speak up for justice, equality, and opportunity. It makes sense for them to do so: they know that the black people who are unknown to the masses of white folk are deserving of the same decency and respect that they are given. Thus, they can leverage their influence and fame on behalf of the black folk whose love and nurture made them stars.

It sears the conscience of many athletes that their fellow black folk are not shown the good treatment they enjoy. But more than survivor guilt compels them to act. These athletes see the contradiction between American ideals of fairness and justice and their arbitrary application to people of color. A black person often has to be a superstar athlete and beloved icon to enjoy only some of the perks that many white folk can take for granted at birth. In an earlier day that lesson might have been clear: after all, the families of black athletes still had to drink from separate water fountains, attend segregated schools, live within the aching echo of black inferiority written into the laws and customs of the land. Those athletes speaking up revealed that they saw how black exceptionalism only went so far. On any given day, the brutal practices of white supremacy could hurt their loved ones. The same is tragically true today.

All of this seems foreign to folk who don't depend on their sports stars or their entertainers to double as part-time spokespeople for the race. Taylor Swift carries no such burden; neither does baseball superstar Bryce Harper. Sure, there is ethnic pride at stake, as there was when Joe DiMaggio made the Italians proud, and Jews exulted in the play of Hank Greenberg and Sandy Koufax. But, despite the undeniable prejudice some of them confronted, none faced the feisty assortment of bigotries that dogged the black athlete's path.

Sadly, the number of athletes speaking out is relatively small. Ali's transformation from pariah to hero was aided by the silence inflicted on him by his disease. Michael Jordan, consciously or not, reversed the order: during his playing days, he was depressingly silent about the injustices that plagued his people, and now, tentatively, he speaks up when the terms are uncontroversial, his reputation safe.

One of the reasons so many athletes have taken after Jordan rather than Ali has little to do with conscience and more to do with the forms such expression might take. Today's black athlete thrives in a time that has shifted from social conscience to social service. They perform humanitarian deeds: visit a sick child at a hospital, lend a hand in building a house, raise money for the relief of hurricane disasters. These are laudable acts—and politically neutral. They risk little of the athlete's reputation, demand very little of his or her political capital.

The stakes of going beyond the public service script are much higher for today's athletes, because far more than compensation for their main jobs is on the table: "good" reputations lead to lucrative endorsement deals and huge financial windfalls as spokespeople for athletic brands with global economic footprints. Athletes who dare challenge the social service paradigm today risk curtailing future paydays. Talking about racial injustice might soil your reputation and nick your N-scores and Q-rating, which measure one's celebrity and brand appeal.

Of course, a punishing paradox is afoot: the very willingness of earlier black athletes to buck trends, speak their minds, and challenge orthodoxy put contemporary black athletes in a golden financial position today. Black baseball player Curt Flood's 1969 challenge to the punishing system of team "ownership" of players led to free agency and billions of dollars for all major leaguers. Spencer Haywood accomplished a similar feat in basketball.

Basketball superstar LeBron James has consistently spoken his mind about race and its consequences in America. Most recently, he spoke out about having racist graffiti scrawled on his Los Angeles home. He appealed to the memory of Emmett Till to make his case. "I think back to Emmet Till's mom actually, and the reason that she had an open casket is because she wanted to show the world what her son went through as far as a hate crime and being black in America."[12] James' winning of two championships in Miami, and then triumphantly returning home to win another championship in Cleveland, has cemented his athletic reputation while enhancing his ability to speak his mind on social issues. He may be chasing Jordan on the court, but away from hoops he bested the legend long ago.

When James announced in 2014 that he was returning home to Cleveland to play basketball, it was in dramatically different fashion from how he had announced his decision four years earlier to leave the Cavaliers. This time James posted an open letter to the *Sports Illustrated* website to tell the world of his plans. In 2010, LeBron had famously announced in a nationally televised special entitled *The Decision* that "I'm taking my talents to South Beach."[13] Those words broke the hearts of Cleveland fans and literally ignited their ire when some of them took to the streets to burn replicas of his jersey. Cavaliers owner Dan Gilbert behaved worst of all, posting to the team's website a scathing letter that lambasted James as a coward, narcissist, traitor, and poor role model. Renowned civil rights activist Jesse Jackson said in 2010 that Gilbert's feelings of betrayal "personify a slave master mentality" and portray the player as "a runaway slave."[14]

Even those who defended James' choice to leave Cleveland condemned *The Decision,* a spectacle that sparked broad ill will. That's where revisionist history meets the distorted lens of the media. There was absolutely *nothing* wrong with the way LeBron left Cleveland. The media and fans that condemn *The Decision* forget that they zealously created the market for it in the year leading up to LeBron's free agency. No matter the conversation—whether it was about a victory or loss, or the local economy in northeast Ohio—it all turned back to one question: will LeBron stay, or will he leave Cleveland?

The media hypocritically made *The Decision* seem like self-evident folly. Yet it had clamored for every bit of information and overdosed on interpreting every LeBron gesture as if parsing the pronouncements of the Pope. After all, he was King James and his kingdom of admirers, as well as his haters, followed his every move. It was this very intense, nearly unmanageable, ravenous, and fanatic desire for LeBron knowledge that led to *The Decision*.

And what did James do with ad revenue from *The Decision*? Gave $2 million in cash, with another million in computers and gear, to 59 Boys & Girls Clubs across America. Narcissism never looked so altruistic. We also can't overlook how James changed the power dynamics of the game of basketball for millionaire players against billionaire owners by taking full advantage of free agency. LeBron was able to hold the world captive because the cards were in his hands, and not, as they usually are, in the hands of owners and their representatives, who often make arbitrary decisions about the future of players with no consultation. In 2014, James and New York Knicks free agent Carmelo Anthony made the league of rich, mostly white male owners sweat it out, waiting to see what 'Bron and 'Melo would do. That's not simply a reversal of fortune; that's a healthy and more egalitarian change of basketball's racial and financial narrative.

LeBron's *Sports Illustrated* letter also revealed him to be a man of transcendent moral courage—an athlete willing to take on leadership. LeBron's letter was virtually a religious document: it teemed with belief in his calling, the economic revival of northeast Ohio, and, above all, a forgiving heart for the undeserved hate he endured following his decision in 2010. Like another King from the dim mists of history who preached the redemption of unearned suffering and the power of forgiveness, LeBron James showed us that one can go home again and make it even better than when one left. Not only has James spoken his mind, he has led the way in offering hope, and enormous aid, through college scholarships to young folk, especially those from his troubled native soil of Akron, Ohio.

The mainstream shift from social conscience to social service has been complemented, and supplemented, by social media, which has afforded athletes an outlet to reach huge audiences directly. They are less likely to be misinterpreted, or misrepresented, if they speak for themselves. Imagine if Muhammad Ali had had Twitter while he battled the U.S. government. Imagine if Hank Aaron had had Facebook as he faced down surly bigots who sought to dissuade him from his pursuit of Babe Ruth's hallowed home run mark.

Imagine if Bill Russell had had Instagram to document his duels with off-court racism in Boston during his still-unmatched championship run. Social media has given players their voices. Seattle Seahawks football champion Michael Bennett can offer his side of how he was brutalized by police; his former teammate Richard Sherman can comment on how "thug" has become the new "N" word for "uppity" black athletes.

Still, digital media, and the black stars it amplifies, cannot escape the analogue vices, deficits, and bigotries that survive technological change and resurface in our day. The same social media that lets LeBron speak lets vile bigots spew their venom. One of them happens to be the most powerful person in the world. The attempt to quarantine black speech to calling plays in the athletic arena rings out in our day from the highest office in the land. What President Trump's Twitter fingers reveal, what his twitchy, apoplectic outrage proves, is that he is, perhaps, the most unpatriotic of all American presidents. But his perverted vision of patriotism cannot stop the efforts of the truly righteous.

Some brave souls may sacrifice their careers to highlight the oppression that everyday black folk confront. Colin Kaepernick's story is in the vein of Ali; it made sense that he was awarded the Muhammad Ali Legacy Award by *Sports Illustrated* in 2017. Global superstar Beyoncé surprised Kaepernick by presenting his award.

Thank you, Colin Kaepernick. Thank you for your selfless heart and your conviction. Thank you for your personal sacrifice. Colin took action with no fear of consequences or repercussion—only hope to change the world for the better, to change perception, to change the way we treat each other, especially people of color. We are still waiting for the world to catch up. It's been said that racism is so American that when we protest racism, some assume we're protesting America. So let's be very clear. Colin has always been very respectful of the individuals who selflessly serve and protect our country and our communities and our families. His message is solely focused on social injustice for historically disenfranchised people. Let's not get that mistaken.[15]

Beyoncé received predictable criticism for her challenge to white innocence and privilege, but, as she has of late, she paid it no mind in exercising her astute political judgment.

Privileged white folk must also use their platforms to challenge inequality. Detroit Pistons coach and president Stan Van Gundy is a courageous man who spoke bluntly about Donald Trump after he was elected, saying that he didn't think "anybody can deny this guy is openly and brazenly racist and misogynistic."[16] Van Gundy argued that we "have just thrown a good part of our population under the bus." More recently, Van Gundy lamented that while "our current president has made the national anthem a divisive issue, the positive is we are now talking about some very important problems. There are serious issues of inequality and injustice in this country," and "I stand with those opposing such bigotry."

San Antonio Spurs coach Gregg Popovich is an outspoken white advocate for white folk acknowledging privilege. Popovich said of his fellow white folk, "We still have no clue of what being born white means,"[17] and he argued that "recent literature" suggests "there is no such thing as whiteness," that "we made it up," and that because "you were born white, you have advantages systemically, culturally . . . People don't want to give it up. Until it's given up, it's not going to be fixed." And Atlanta Falcons owner Arthur Blank told me that he was quite sympathetic to the social issues that black folk face and that black players express, and that, even more, he was interested in generating solutions to the problems that plague our people and nation. Van Gundy, Popovich, and Blank are markedly different than most of their white peers. They have courageously attempted to provoke other white coaches and team owners to grapple with the racial cauldron in the nation and to leverage their authority as prominent sports figures to encourage conversation and constructive practices to yield genuine change.

These men are true patriots, true lovers of democracy, who desire to see substantive social transformation in our country. That cannot happen without agitation and resistance, without protest and uncomfortable moments of reckoning. Kaepernick's legacy resides far beyond the gridiron he deserves to play on; it resides in the spiral of social awareness and public conscience that his poignant protest has unleashed. Like Robinson, and Ali, and so many others, his inspiring example rallies many more to muster the courage to face down oppression in our land.

AFTER THE MEETING

RESURRECTION FOR RFK

If Martin Luther King Jr.'s martyrdom instantly transformed him from social pariah to high priest of American moral possibility, then Robert F. Kennedy's assassination remade him in the image of an ideal self he labored hard to craft in the last few years of his life. When Sirhan Sirhan shot Kennedy on June 5, 1968, two months and a day after King's murder, the course of American history was once again violently changed. The prospects for racial healing that Kennedy's evolved thinking had promised were bitterly dashed.

Bobby had come a long way from his earliest days in the public eye. After Jack's assassination, Bobby resigned as attorney general to become a New York senator. He began to delve far more deeply into the urban crisis he was made to see brewing when he met with

Baldwin and friends. Although Bobby and Baldwin and his peers came away from that meeting deeming it a disaster, it liberated Bobby from his political pragmatism. Bobby began to walk in the shoes of the dispossessed, to take in their stories up close, to witness the mangled faces of babies bitten by rats, to smell the social death that lingered in the air after flames settled into embers and eventually lined the streets with soot. If he had learned anything from his brutal encounter with Baldwin, it was that, whether he wanted to or not, he had to listen to the unfiltered rage that tore at the hearts and minds of millions of Negroes.

Bobby learned to see race as more than a political matter and began to see racism as Baldwin and his group had urged him to see it: as moral rot at the heart of the American empire. "I have seen the people of the black ghetto," Bobby said on March 18, 1968, a couple of days after he announced his candidacy for the presidency, "listening to ever greater promises of equality and of justice, as they sit in the same decaying schools and huddled in the same filthy rooms—without heat—warding off the cold and warding off the rats. If we believe that we, as Americans, are bound together by a common concern for each other, then an urgent national priority is upon us. We must begin to end the disgrace of this other America."[1]

When King was murdered in Memphis, Bobby was profoundly changed, perhaps feeling as Baldwin felt after King's death—that he was the last witness left, the last one to give convincing testimony to the American public about the wages of racial sin and the righteous path to political redemption. When Bobby calmed and consoled a black crowd in Indianapolis to whom he announced King's death, he offered eloquent testimony about the need to move away from polarization and to make "an effort to understand, to go beyond these rather difficult times."[2] Bobby pleaded with the crowd that what "we need in the United States is not division; what we need in the United States is not hatred; what we need in the United States is not violence or lawlessness, but love and wisdom, and compassion toward one another, and a feeling of justice towards those who still suffer within our country, whether they be white or they be black."

Bobby contended that "the vast majority of white people and the vast majority of black people in this country want to live together, want to improve the quality of our life, and want justice for all human beings who abide in our land." That may not have been any truer then than it is now—King in his later years believed that "most Americans are unconscious racists"[3]—but it was important that a national political figure utter those words in unrepentant optimism and durable hopefulness. We are now living with a political leader so corrupted by an incurable doubt about the goodness of his fellow citizens that his disbelief in our creeds amounts to a chilling renunciation of American ideals. Bobby nurtured such beliefs as a sublime political reflex; Trump undercuts them as a subversive political reactionary.

This is not to say that Bobby had been flawless, that he had got past his callous ways. At the hotel after his moving speech about King, Bobby made what appeared to be a heartless exclamation about the fallen leader's assassination. "After all, it's not the greatest tragedy in the history of the Republic."[4] Even though he called Coretta Scott King and arranged to have King's body flown back to Atlanta, Bobby didn't really mourn a man he'd never been especially close to or even fond of. King grew to believe that Bobby should be supported and respected; Bobby distrusted King and seemed stricken by guilt for wiretapping him. And yet Bobby was ushered by history to King's side to partner in the work of racial justice.

By the time Bobby perished, the policy he had once touted was brilliantly implemented by his arch nemesis Lyndon Baines Johnson. Bobby had become known as a racial healer, even a prophet of sorts and, ironically, a witness for the invisible poor. He had come to embody the moral message of Baldwin and his fellow witnesses. Baldwin may have thought that their meeting was useless; Clark may have written it off as a resounding failure, just as Bobby had, but in the end, Bobby became what he couldn't understand at the time: a fierce witness to the suffering of black people.

Bobby had only just begun; his martyrdom made him more in death than he had been in life. His death brought him closer to an image of the racial ombudsman he had aspired to be, an image that still inspires us to be compassionate toward the most marginal members of our society.

Bobby's achievements have continued after death as his memory stretches the horizons of our sight far beyond the bigotries that blind us. Bobby is bigger now than he has ever been. A meeting with a few angry black folk more than fifty years ago taught him a valuable lesson about listening to what you don't want to hear. It is a lesson we must learn today if we are to overcome our differences and embrace a future as bright as our dreams allow.

EVEN IF

WAKANDA. FOREVER

I beg you, as the youth are wont to say these days, please don't judge me, but I've got a confession: I believe that most of the ills that I address in this book—the racism, the sexism, the homophobia—can be engaged, if not relieved, if we, yes, reread Baldwin and scores of really smart black intellectuals, including Robin D. G. Kelley and Farah Jasmine Griffin, and if we elect good politicians like Kamala Harris, Andrea Jenkins, Ras Baraka, and Eric Holder, and if we listen to great artists like Jay-Z and Beyoncé, and Kendrick and Rapsody. But—and here's where I beseech your understanding—they might all be solved if we all took a trip to Wakanda. I know, I know, it's cheesy that I'm capitulating to the hype around a blockbuster superhero film, surrendering the high aesthetic moral ground to a piece of popular entertainment that may sully the intellectual credibility of all the BIG IDEAS I've grappled with here. But you couldn't be more wrong! Everything about *Black Panther* is right, timely, and, dare I say, prophetic—even black prophecy at its best—a visual witness to the aspirations and ideals we harbor in our black chests when we let our imaginations roam free.

But let's be honest, the appeal of Wakanda is also its shame: that in this day, in this age, it should even be necessary for black folk to be so hungry for representation that we flock to the movie theater by the millions to see on screen a fictional version of what our society can't provide us every day—a place where race is not an issue and our blackness is taken for granted.

Yes, it is true, but it is also grievous, that in a world where Martin Luther King has spoken, where Billie Holiday has sung, where James Baldwin has written, where Sidney Poitier has acted, where Muhammad Ali has boxed, where Harriet Tubman has escaped, where George Washington Carver has invented, where Barbara Jordan has politicked, where Julius Erving has dunked, where Katherine Dunham has danced, where Serena Williams has smashed, where Toni Morrison has created, where Barack Obama has presided, that it is *still* necessary to proclaim our genius or assert our humanity or argue for our beauty, our dignity, our worth, our simple ability to make it through the day without a single policeman using his baton to beat us or his taser to stun us or his gun to shoot us.

We love Wakanda because Wakanda loves us.

Wakanda is the name of our paradise and possibility.

Wakanda is the place of our unapologetic blackness, a blackness that is beautiful and ugly, that is uplifting and destructive, that is peaceful and violent, that is, in a word, human in all of its glory and grief, with no special pleading for its virtue, no excuse made for its wickedness, except that wickedness exists, and in its existence, we find it necessary to address it, to fight it, to remove it, but not to defend ourselves against the belief that it represents all black people.

Wakanda is black all over and everywhere and wherever its blackness exists there exists, too, the infinite possibilities, and any and all options available to the human being—the magic and madness, the belief and cynicism, the positive and negative, all of it there, together, in one place, not segregated or artificially divided, so we can say "Here is what's good about us, and there is what's bad about us, because neither exhausts who we are. We are always, perpetually, more than what it seems we are."

In Wakanda, we finally get the chance to just be—like white folk can, and do, every day of their lives.

Yes, it's true, white folk have a Wakanda, too, but its name is different, because, even though it's chock full of myths, ideals, tales, and potions, it actually exists in real time, with real flesh and blood, with real cities and realities attached to it.

Its name is democracy. Its name is Iowa, or New York.

Its name is bread, and car, and air, and speech, and school, and law and travel and society; in other words, whatever and wherever whiteness exists and is seen as normal and necessary, as usual, as taken for granted, as presumed, as invisible and unaccountable and, therefore, not necessary to be named Wakanda. Fantasy ain't needed when reality already provides what fiction aims for.

Wakanda is necessary for us because our black lives are seen as anything but. Wakanda matters because black lives don't.

We went to see *Black Panther* time and again because time and again we had to remind ourselves that the denial of our beauty, time and again, is not real. That what is real is what we see projected as a fantasy, but which we know, in our hearts, in our black bodies, to be true. We are that great. We are that intelligent. We do love science. (It's never been science that scares us; it's been scientists who pervert knowledge to justify our inferiority or our deaths. Ugh. Enough of that. This ain't Kansas, Dorothy, and yes, Kansas, at least for Dorothy and millions of others, is a white

Wakanda.) We do love our skin. Our hair. Our noses. We love the way the camera loves us in Wakanda. The way it lavishes visual praise on our black elegance.

Wakanda exists because what we should have is not here. Justice. Truth. Love.

Wakanda exists because for centuries we have struggled to imagine ourselves as the arbiters of our destiny when we are unfettered by hate and fear.

In Wakanda our battles have to do with the big ideas and truths that all folk confront on their human journey.

In Wakanda there is no second-guessing ourselves, our smarts, our looks, our bodies, except for the normal reasons and insecurities we all possess.

We keep going back to see Wakanda because the celebration of our blackness, the pageantry of our blackness, the hipness of our blackness, the rituals and rites and reasons of our blackness, the depth and breadth of our blackness, its wily widths, its poignant parameters, its monumental measures, are all there for us to see, to take in with all of our senses.

Wakanda is Black Love.

Wakanda is Black Brilliance.

Wakanda is Black Blackness.

Not a blackness manufactured by others to satisfy their lust for our coolness, our suave, our earthiness, our grittiness, our sensuality, our sexiness. It is a blackness that is black enough to be black when it matters most, when no one is looking, when no one is judging, when no one cares more than they should, or less than they ought, when blackness, in all of its splendid blackness, simply is.

Wakanda is so appealing because having to explain ourselves to those who doubt us—doubt our minds, doubt our motives, doubt our goodness, doubt our undoubtable hugeness, doubt our epic and oracular and spectacular blackness—plain wears us out.

Wakanda is our weariness rejected and made unnecessary.

Wakanda is where microaggressions go to die.

Wakanda is a Fannie Lou Hamer Holiday where being sick and tired of being sick and tired is retired.

We are tired of explaining why it's not cool to touch our hair.

We are tired of explaining why our hair looks different than yours.

We are tired of explaining why our hair isn't always long and straight.

We are tired of explaining why natural hair is a choice we make to combat the belief that the only "good" hair is white hair.

We are tired of explaining why the weaves we wear are more than extensions of our locks, but are extensions, too, of our fierce desire to style ourselves a new reality.

We are tired of telling you that white privilege is real.

We are tired of telling you that white people get away with shit that black people could never dream of.

Hence Wakanda.

We are tired of telling you for the billionth time that, no, white people are not the victims of racism more than black or brown people are.

We are tired of telling you that affirmative action is something you benefitted from for centuries except it had another name for you. That name is living.

We are tired of telling you that our kids are viewed differently than yours, in ways far worse than you can imagine.

We are tired of telling you that things your kids get reprimanded for our kids get remanded for.

We are tired of telling you that black folk with degrees often don't have the same shot at a job as white folk with criminal convictions. Think. About. That.

We are tired of telling you that doing the same crime as a white person often lands black folk in hotter water with longer sentences under far worse conditions.

We are tired of telling you that we are not thugs.

We are tired of telling you that we are not criminals.

We are tired of telling you that Trayvon did not deserve to die at the hands of a racist vigilante who killed him because he is a coward and the most flagrant example of how you protect vicious people and turn their guilt into unconvincing innocence.

Wakanda is where Trayvon reigns as a King. As a Warrior. Most important, as a Man. Because he made it past a youth that is forever in peril in a culture that doesn't prize our breathing.

Wakanda is our insistence that we will choose how to be black.

Wakanda is our insistence that we will choose what to be black about.

Hint: everything.

Wakanda is our refusal to let others tell us what is important to us. About us. For us.

Wakanda is our refusal to anymore pretend that what is happening to us in the real world, in real time, is really real. *This* is the illusion. This—this notion that oppression is natural, that violence is inevitable, that hate is normal, that whiteness is a birthright, that subordination is good, that empire is a goal, that control is a virtue—this is what is unnatural, false, fake, undesirable, should be banned and bashed and banished.

Wakanda is our "told you so" that black films can do well here and abroad. That black superheroes can be loved by black folk and others at the same time. That white folk can watch us just like we watch you, when there are no black characters, and yet we still empathize, and care, and cry, and identify with you.

Wakanda is what we are when we are done with explanations of our blackness and exult instead in exclamations of our blackness.

Is it sad that all of this was inspired by a movie? In a way, perhaps, but then works of art have always inspired us to see ourselves in ways that aren't permitted when ruthless and narrow versions of reality pass for truth.

From this moment on let Wakanda be our vibrant affirmation, our joyous "amen."

You like something black? Wakanda.

Our rhythms excite you? Wakanda.

Our brains bring you to the edge? Wakanda.

Our love can redeem this world? Wakanda.

Our hunger for justice can free the rest of the world too? Wakanda.

Wakanda is the Wakanda of today and forever? Wakanda.

So, yes, it may seem silly, or kitschy, or needy, or downright desperate. Makes no difference. Wakanda exists in our minds and souls because our minds and souls have never existed as they should in the minds and souls of those who look on us with contempt or pity or derision or indifference.

Wakanda is our pledge to never let any of that determine how we see or love ourselves.

Agree?

Wakanda. Forever.

Acknowledgments

No book is produced without the cooperation of many good folk. I want to thank my agent—really my intellectual co-conspirator—Tanya McKinnon, an extraordinary thinker who, more than the usual duties of her office, helps guide the intellectual imaginations, as well as the careers, of her fortunate clients. She is simply the best in the nation.

I am also grateful to my St. Martin's editor, Elisabeth Dyssegaard, the best editor one might find, a gifted visionary and relentless perfectionist who demands the best of her writers, down to the last seconds before the book appears. I'm thankful for her refusal of anything but the best one—I—can do. Shout outs to my St. Martin's family, including Sally Richardson, Don Weisberg, Jennifer Enderlin, George Witte, Martin Quinn, and Laura Clark, for all their uplifting belief in, and support of, my work.

Alan Bradshaw, a managing editor at St. Martin's, offered wonderful, conscientious guidance and superb attention to every detail to make certain that the book you hold in your hand looks and reads as fluidly as possible. Thanks, too, to copy editor, Jennifer Simington, who worked diligently to shape the manuscript with an eye for the literary grace to which all authors aspire. Thanks also to designer Meryl Levavi, typesetter Letra Libre, jacket designer David Baldeosingh Rotstein, production manager Lena Shekhter, and proofreaders Donna Cherry and Lisa Davis. Thanks as well for the wonderful publicity work of Gabrielle Gantz.

Micah English did yeoman's work as my research assistant while serving as my tremendous teaching assistant, really my co-teacher, for my Georgetown courses, quickly and comprehensively engaging a huge body of thought and retrieving articles and books that were critical to this enterprise. She is an enormously talented thinker and budding producer as well. Arelia Johnson packed up her children and headed to the Schomburg Library to find and retrieve vital original documents, while Sekou Sankofa expeditiously rounded up elusive documents. They are both Howard University's finest. Thanks to the good folk at the JFK Library and the Schomburg Library for their help, and to Sara Blair for a last-minute overnight gift of her book *Harlem Crossroads* when I was at the wire.

Thanks to my *Raw Word* family: our great EPs Ice-T and Andre Jetmir (thanks for your wonderful advocacy and great support) and my co-hosts Claudia Jordan and Dan Ratner (thank you so much for your incredible and timely support, my friend). And thanks to my groomer and stylist, Marvin "Marv the Barb" Church, the world's best barber, and Ms. Carolyn Brown, who squires me in a marvelous manner.

I'm grateful to the remarkable group of artists and activists who sat for interviews for this book, including Harry Belafonte (thanks for the amazing blurb), Clarence Jones, Muhammad Ali, Jesse Williams, Lin-Manuel Miranda, Leslie Odom, Jr., Daveed Diggs, Renee Elise Goldsberry, Keegan-Michael Key, Jordan Peele (congrats on the well-deserved Oscar!), Hillary Clinton, Chadwick Boseman (Wakanda, Forever), Andrea Jenkins, Kamala Harris, Adam Walinsky, Tarana Burke, Frederick Haynes, Avery Jackson, Julius Jones, Arthur Blank, and Jerome Smith.

I am profoundly grateful to MJJP—Michelle is a committed principal, brilliant intellectual, and gifted manager of my social media interventions. Thanks for the incredible work, and for the love and devotion.

And, as always, I'm thankful to the Dyson clan for the love, support, and encouragement over the years. My mother, Addie Mae Dyson, is our loving matriarch. Everett Dyson-Bey (hope to see you home soon), Gregory, and Brian are my wonderful brothers.

Michael, Mwata, and Maisha are my amazing children, and their children Layla, Mosi, and Maxem my lovely grandchildren.

I am grateful for the incredible sacrifice, intellectual partnership and enormous support and love over all the years of the family's guiding spirit and loving matriarch, Rev. Marcia Dyson. Congratulations on your forthcoming memoir, *Irreverent: The Memoir of a Grown-Ass Woman*. I know it will be a great literary work and a bestseller.

Finally (along with my late cousin Oscar Madison), my oldest, beloved brother, Anthony—1957–2017—died as I wrote this book, and he is sorely missed every single day—R.I.P., my courageous guide and pioneer in so much of my life.

Notes

The Martyrs

1. Martin Luther King, Jr., "I've Been to the Mountaintop," in Clayborne Carson, editor, *A Call to Conscience: The Landmark Speeches of Dr. Martin Luther King, Jr.* (New York: Grand Central Publishing, reprint, 2002), p. 207.
2. James Baldwin, "Malcolm and Martin," *Esquire,* April, 1972, p. 201.
3. Ibid.

The Meeting

1. Layhmond Robinson, "Robert Kennedy Consults Negroes Here About North," *The New York Times,* May 25, 1963.
2. Arthur M. Schlesinger, *Robert Kennedy and His Times* (New York: Houghton Mifflin Company, 1978, 2002), pp. 328–30.
3. The following paragraphs are informed by Evan Thomas, *Robert Kennedy: His Life* (New York: Simon & Schuster, reprint, 2002), especially pp. 240–262.
4. Michael Cohen, "Bobby Kennedy: Democratic Apostate, Political Opportunist, Liberal Idealist . . ." *The Guardian,* June 6, 2013, https://www.theguardian.com/comment isfree/2013/jun/06/robert-kennedy-assassination-anni versary (accessed 2/27/18).
5. Thomas Chatterton Williams, "Breaking into James Baldwin's House," October 28, 2015, https://www.new yorker.com/news/news-desk/breaking-into-james-bald wins-house (accessed 2/27/18).

6. James Baldwin (1963, May 12). Telegram to Attorney General Robert Kennedy, Box 2, Folder 2, Robert Park Mills Papers, Harry Ransom Humanities Research Center, University of Texas at Austin.
7. Jean Stein and George Plimpton, *American Journey: The Times of Robert Kennedy* (New York: Harcourt Brace Jovanovich, 1970), pp. 118–119.
8. Robert Kennedy, recorded interview #7 by Anthony Lewis, December 22, 1964, 585, John F. Kennedy Library Oral History Program; Edwin O. Guthman and Jeffrey Shulman, editors, *Robert Kennedy: In His Own Words: The Unpublished Recollections of the Kennedy Years* (New York: Bantam, 1988); Stein and Plimpton, *American Journey.*
9. This point is made in the brilliant and hugely insightful Tracy Heather Strain documentary on Hansberry, *Lorraine Hansberry: Sighted Eyes/Feeling Heart,* PBS, January 19, 2018.
10. The account of the meeting, including quotations cited in the ensuing pages, draws from Jean Stein and George Plimpton, *American Journey,* pp. 118-125; Harry Belafonte, *My Song* (New York: Random House, 2011), pp. 265-269; Lena Horne and Richard Schickel, *Lena* (New York: Harper & Row, 1965, 1986), pp. 275-281; James Campbell, *Talking at the Gates: A Life of James Baldwin* (New York: Penguin Books, 1991), pp. 163-171; Evan Thomas, *Robert Kennedy: His Life* (New York: Simon and Schuster, 2000), pp. 242–246; Guthman and Shulman, *Robert Kennedy: In His Own Words*; Schlesinger, *Robert Kennedy and His Times*; Todd Saucedo, "The Fire Within: The Baldwin Meeting and the Evolution of the Kennedy Administration's Approach to Civil Rights," Master's thesis, University of Central Florida, 2007; Steven Levingston, *Kennedy and King: The President, The Pastor, and the Battle Over Civil Rights* (New York: Hachette Books, 2017); Carol Polsgrove, *Divided Minds: Intellectuals and the Civil Rights Movement* (New York: W. W. Norton, 1st edition, 2001); Larry Tye, *Bobby Kennedy: The Making of a Liberal Icon* (New York: Random House, 2016); Harris Wofford, *Of Kennedys & Kings: Making Sense of the Sixties* (New York: Farrar, Straus, Giroux, 1980); Victor S. Navasky, *Kennedy Justice* (New York: Atheneum, 1971); Fern Eckman, *The Furious Passage of James Baldwin* (New York: Lippincott, 1966); David Leeming, *James Baldwin: A Biography* (New York:

Knopf, 1994); William J. Weatherby, *James Baldwin: Artist on Fire* (New York: Donald Fine, 1989).

11. Guthman and Shulman, *Robert Kennedy: In His Own Words,* p. 224.

12. James Baldwin, Emile Capouya, Lorraine Hansberry, Nat Hentoff, Langston Hughes, and Alfred Kazin, "The Negro in American Culture," *CrossCurrents* 11, no. 3 (Summer 1961): 205.

13. Stein, *American Journey,* p. 119.

14. Ibid.

15. Ibid.

16. Thomas, *Robert Kennedy,* p. 244.

17. Guthman and Shulman, *Robert Kennedy: In His Own Words,* p. 224.

18. Ibid., p. 125.

19. Thomas, *Robert Kennedy,* p. 245.

20. Saucedo, "The Fire Within," p. 2.

21. Levingston, *Kennedy and King,* p. 392; Thomas, *Robert Kennedy,* p. 245.

22. Edwin Guthman, *We Band of Brothers* (New York: Harper & Row, 1971), p. 221.

The Politicians

1. This first section is informed by Robert G. Parkinson, *The Common Cause: Creating Race and Nation in the American Revolution* (Chapel Hill: University of North Carolina Press, 2016), pp. 1–21, 185–263.

2. Steven Levingston, *Kennedy and King: The President, The Pastor, and the Battle Over Civil Rights* (New York: Hachette Books, 2017), pp. 80–82.

3. Ibid., pp. 310–11.

4. Michael Eric Dyson, *I May Not Get There with You: The True Martin Luther King, Jr.* (reprint, New York: Free Press, 2001), pp. 30–50.

5. Jose A. DelReal, "African Americans Are 'in the worst shape they've ever been,' Trump says in North Carolina," *The Washington Post,* September 20, 2016, https://www.washingtonpost.com/news/post-politics/wp/2016/09/20/african-americans-are-in-the-worst-shape-they ve-ever-been-trump-says-in-north-carolina/?utm_term =.b7e5bb329170 (accessed 2/27/18).

6. Evelyn Rupert, "Obama: Trump Missed History Lessons on Slavery, Jim Crow," *The Hill,* September 17, 2016, http://thehill.com/blogs/blog-briefing-room/news

/296493-obama-trump-missed-history-lessons-on-slav
ery-jim-crow (accessed 2/27/18).

7. Michael Arceneaux, "Bernie Sanders Still Says Class
Is More Important Than Race. He Is Still Wrong,"
The Guardian, November 22, 2016, https://www.the
guardian.com/commentisfree/2016/nov/22/bernie-san
ders-identity-politics-class-race-debate (accessed 2/27/
18).

8. Libby Nelson, "'Why we voted for Donald Trump': David Duke Explains the White Supremacist Charlottesville Protests." *Vox,* August 12, 2017, https://www.vox
.com/2017/8/12/16138358/charlottesville-protests-david
-duke-kkk (accessed 2/27/18).

9. Charles Blow, "The Lowest White Man," *The New York
Times,* January 11, 2018, https://www.nytimes.com/2018
/01/11/opinion/trump-immigration-white-supremacy
.html (accessed 2/27/18).

10. Maggie Astor, "John Kelly Pins Civil War on a 'Lack of
Ability to Compromise,'" *The New York Times,* October
31, 2017, https://www.nytimes.com/2017/10/31/us/john
-kelly-civil-war.html (accessed 2/27/18).

11. Adam Bernstein, "Shelby Foote Dies," *Washington
Post,* June 29, 2005, https://www.washingtonpost.com
/archive/local/2005/06/29/shelby-foote-dies/93c8d5
a5-77bf-4797-83d8-185f700ed85b/?utm_term=.81b046
b397d4 (accessed 3/15/18).

12. "The Split Personality of Ken Burns's 'The Civil War,'"
Civil War Memory, August 31, 2015, http://cwmemory
.com/2015/08/31/the-split-personality-of-ken-burnss
-the-civil-war/ (accessed 2/27/18).

13. "Full Transcript and Video: Joe Kennedy Delivers Democratic Response to State of the Union," New York Times,
Jan. 31, 2018. https://www.nytimes.com/2018/01/31/us/
politics/transcript-joe-kennedy-democratic-response.
html.

The Artists

1. Karla V. Zelaya, "Sweat the Technique: Visible-izing
Praxis Through Mimicry in Phillis Wheatley's 'On Being
Brought from Africa to America.'" Doctoral disserta-
tion, University of Massachusetts, Amherst, September,
2015.

2. James Baldwin, *James Baldwin: Collected Essays* (New
York: Library of America, 1998), p. 669. For an excellent
exploration of Baldwin as artist, see Ed Pavlic, *Who Can
Afford to Improvise? James Baldwin and Black Music,*

the Lyric and the Listeners (New York: Oxford University Press, 2015).

3. Ibid., p. 687.

4. Much of this section, including quotes, draws from Judith Smith, *Becoming Belafonte: Black Artist, Public Radical* (reprint, Austin: University of Texas Press, 2016).

5. Simon Callow, "The Emperor Robeson," *The New York Review of Books,* February 8, 2018, http://www.nybooks .com/articles/2018/02/08/emperor-paul-robeson/ (accessed 2/27/18).

6. Smith, *Becoming Belafonte,* p. 145.

7. Ibid., p. 141.

8. "Belafonte Won't Back Down from Powell Slave Reference," CNN.com, October 16, 2002, http://www.cnn.com /2002/US/10/15/belafonte.powell/ (accessed 2/27/18).

9. Tamar Gottesman, "Beyonce Wants to Change the Conversation," *Elle,* April 4, 2016, https://www.elle.com/fash ion/a35286/beyonce-elle-cover-photos/ (accessed 2/28 /18).

10. Walter A. McDougall identifies hustling as the central motif of American culture in his *Freedom Just Around the Corner: A New American History 1585-1828* (New York: Perennial, 2005).

11. Sara Blair, *Harlem Crossroads: Black Writers and the Photograph in the Twentieth Century* (Princeton, NJ: Princeton University Press, 2007), pp. 160-223.

12. Thomas Chatterton Williams, "Breaking Into James Baldwin's House," *The New Yorker,* October 28, 2015, https://www.newyorker.com/news/news-desk/break ing-into-james-baldwins-house (accessed 2/27/18).

13. Darryl Pinckney, "Riffs," *The New York Review of Books,* January 11, 2001, http://www.nybooks.com/ar ticles/2001/01/11/riffs/ (accessed 2/27/18).

14. Kevin Mumford, "Opening the Restricted Box: Lorraine Hansberry's Lesbian Writing," OutHistory.org, http:// outhistory.org/exhibits/show/lorraine-hansberry/les bian-writing (accessed 2/27/18).

15. Lorraine Hansberry, "Interview with Lorraine Hansberry by Studs Terkel," radio interview with Studs Terkel, broadcast on WFMT Radio, Chicago, Illinois, May 12, 1959. Transcript reprinted in "Make New Sounds: Studs Terkel Interviews Lorraine Hansberry," *American Theater* (November 1984): 6.

16. Devon Ivie, "Beyoncé Hails 'Selfless' Colin Kaepernick During Muhammad Ali Legacy Award Speech," *W Magazine,* December 6, 2017, https://www.wmagazine.com

/story/beyonce-colin-kaepernick-muhammad-ali-legacy
-award-speech (accessed 2/27/18).

The Intellectuals

1. Kenneth B. Clark, *Pathos of Power* (New York: Harper, 1974), p. 27.
2. Marvin Elkoff, "Everybody Knows His Nme," *Esquire,* August 1964, pp. 59–64.
3. Benjamin Anastas, "Teaching the Controversy: James Baldwin and Richard Wright in the Ferguson Era," *The New Republic,* May 25, 2015, https://newrepublic.com /article/121844/teaching-james-baldwin-and-richard -wright-ferguson-era (accessed 2/27/18).
4. Harold Cruse, *The Crisis of the Negro Intellectual* (New York: NYRB Classics, 1967, 2005), p. 194.
5. Elkoff, "Everybody Knows His Name."
6. Nathan Glazer, "Liberalism and the Negro: A Round-Table Discussion," *Commentary,* March 1, 1964, https:// www.commentarymagazine.com/articles/liberal ism-the-negro-a-round-table-discussion/ (accessed 4/1/ 18).
7. Jordan Elgrably, "James Baldwin, The Art of Fiction No. 78," *The Paris Review* (Spring 1984), https://www.the parisreview.org/interviews/2994/james-baldwin-the -art-of-fiction-no-78-james-baldwin (accessed 2/27/18).
8. James Baldwin, *James Baldwin: Collected Essays* (New York: Library of America, 1998), p. 18; Charles H. Nichols, editor, *Arna Bontemps-Langston Hughes Letters: 1925-1967* (New York: Dodd, Mead & Company, 1980), pp. 406, 408.
9. Eldridge Cleaver, *Soul on Ice* (McHenry, Illinois: Delta, 16th ed., 1999), p. 124.
10. James Baldwin, *James Baldwin: Collected Essays* (New York: Library of America, 1998), p. 459.
11. Concepción de León, "Ta-Nehisi Coates and the Making of a Public Intellectual," *The New York Times,* https:// www.nytimes.com/2017/09/29/books/ta-nehisi-coates -we-were-eight-years-in-power.html (accessed 2/27/18).
12. Dr. Cornel West, "In Defense of James Baldwin," Facebook status update, July 16, 2015, https://www.facebook .com/drcornelwest/posts/10155807310625111 (accessed 2/27/18).
13. Cornel West, "Ta-Nehisi Coates Is the Neoliberal Face of the Black Freedom Struggle," *The Guardian,* December

17, 2017, https://www.theguardian.com/commentisfree/2017/dec/17/ta-nehisi-coates-neoliberal-black-struggle-cornel-west (accessed 2/27/18).

14. Cornel West, "Tavis Smiley, Cornel West on the 2012 Election & Why Calling Obama 'Progressive' Ignores His Record," *Democracy Now!,* November 9, 2012 https://www.democracynow.org/2012/11/9/tavis_smiley_cornel_west_on_the (accessed 2/27/18).

15. Thomas Frank, "Cornel West, 'He posed as a progressive and turned out to be counterfeit. We ended up with a Wall Street presidency, a drone presidency,'" *Salon,* August 8, 2014, https://www.salon.com/2014/08/24/cornel_west_he_posed_as_a_progressive_and_turned_out_to_be_counterfeit_we_ended_up_with_a_wall_street_presidency_a_drone_presidency/ (accessed 2/27/18).

16. David Remnick, "The Oracle," *The New Yorker,* November 2, 2009, https://www.newyorker.com/magazine/2009/11/02/the-oracle-3 (accessed 2/27/18).

17. Frank, "Cornel West."

18. See my *The Black Presidency: Barack Obama and the Politics of Race in America* (New York: Houghton Mifflin Harcourt Publishing Company, 2016), esp. pp. 154–187.

19. Hugh Muir, "Cornel West: 'They say I'm un-American,'" *The Guardian,* May 13, 2013, https://www.theguardian.com/politics/2013/may/13/cornel-west-they-say-i-am-unamerican (accessed 2/27/18).

20. Cornel West, *Brother West: Living and Loving Out Loud* (New York: SmileyBooks, 2009), p. 231.

21. Cornel West, *Ethical Dimensions of Marxist Thought* (New York: NYU Press, 1991), p. xxviii.

22. Cornel West and Christ Buschendorf, *Black Prophetic Fire* (Boston: Beacon Press, 2014), p. 1.

23. Ibid., p. 92.

24. Richard Lischer, *The Preacher King: Martin Luther King, Jr. and the Word that Moved America* (New York: Oxford, 1997), pp. 170–171.

25. Jamil Smith, "'A certain fear of free black men'" *MSNBC,* May 18, 2011, http://www.msnbc.com/rachel-maddow-show/certain-fear-free-black-men (accessed 2/27/18).

26. Jonathan Alter, *The Center Holds: Obama and His Enemies* (New York: Simon & Schuster, 2013), p. 271.

27. Stephen Steinberg, *The Ethnic Myth: Race, Ethnicity, and Class in America* (Boston: Beacon Press, 1995, 2001), pp. 127–128.

28. Cornel West, *Race Matters* (Boston: Beacon Press, 1993, 2001, 2017), p. 18.

29. Ibid., p. 17.

30. Lischer, *The Preacher King,* p. 30.

31. James Baldwin, *No Name in the Street* (New York: Random House, 1972), p. 172.

The Activists 1

1. Jean Stein and George Plimpton, *American Journey: The Times of Robert Kennedy* (New York: Harcourt Brace Jovanovich, 1970), pp. 118–119.

2. Lisa Rosset, *James Baldwin* (Langhorne, Pennsylvania: Chelsea House, 1990) p. 139.

3. Carol Polsgrove, *Divided Minds: Intellectuals and the Civil Rights Movement* (New York: W. W. Norton; 1st edition, 2001).

4. Edwin Guthman, *We Band of Brothers* (New York: Harper & Row, 1971).

5. William Goldsmith, *The Growth of Presidential Power* (New York: Chelsea House, 1974), p.1665.

6. James Baldwin, *The Price of the Ticket: Collected Nonfiction, 1948–1985* (New York: St. Martin's Press, 1985), p. 250.

7. Stein and Plimpton, *American Journey,* pp. 118–125.

8. Dan Merica, "Black Lives Matter Videos, Clinton Campaign Reveal Details of Meeting," *CNN,* August 18, 2015, https://www.cnn.com/2015/08/18/politics/hillary-clinton-black-lives-matter-meeting/index.html (accessed 2/27/18).

9. Robin D. G. Kelley, "What Does Black Lives Matter Want?" *Boston Review,* August 17, 2016, http://bostonreview.net/books-ideas/robin-d-g-kelley-movement-black-lives-vision (accessed 2/27/18).

10. Emily Alpert Reyes, "Mayor's Return to Church Where Protesters Disrupted Him Is Scuttled," *Los Angeles Times,* October 25, 2015, http://www.latimes.com/local/california/la-me-mayor-church-20151026-story.html (accessed 2/27/18).

11. Sabrina Siddiqui, "Black Lives Matter Protest Interrupts Clinton Speech on Criminal Justice," *The Guardian,* October 30, 2015, https://www.theguardian.com/us-news/2015/oct/30/black-lives-matter-protest-interrupts-hillary-clinton (accessed 2/27/18).

12. Bernard L. Fraga, Sean McElwee, Jesse Rhodes, and Brian Schaffner, "Why Did Trump Win? More

Whites—and Fewer Blacks—Actually Voted," *The Washington Post,* May 8, 2017, https://www.washingtonpost.com/news/monkey-cage/wp/2017/05/08/why-did-trump-win-more-whites-and-fewer-blacks-than-normal-actually-voted/?utm_term=.f01cfacaac1e (accessed 2/27/18).

13. Charles D. Ellison, "Black Voter Turnout: A Look at the Numbers," *Philadelphia Tribune,* November 12, 2016, http://www.phillytrib.com/news/black-voter-turnout-a-look-at-the-numbers/article_49d1aed9-76be-550e-b063-15ad7639dc97.html (accessed 4/19/18); Jens Manuel Krogstad and Mark Hugo Lopez, "Black Voter Turnout Fell in 2016, Even as a Record Number of Americans Cast Ballots," Pew Research Center, FACTANK, May 12, 2017, http://www.pewresearch.org/fact-tank/2017/05/12/black-voter-turnout-fell-in-2016-even-as-a-record-number-of-americans-cast-ballots/ (accessed 4/19/18); United States Census, "Voting Rate for the Non-Hispanic Black Population Dropped in the 2016 Presidential Election," May 10, 2017, https://www.census.gov/newsroom/press-releases/2017/cb17-tps45-voting-rates.html (accessed 4/19/18).

14. Kate Philips, "Clinton Touts White Support," *The New York Times,* May 8, 2008, https://thecaucus.blogs.nytimes.com/2008/05/08/clinton-touts-white-support/ (accessed 2/27/18).

15. Sarah Wheaton, "Clinton's Civil Rights Lesson," *The New York Times,* January 7, 2008, https://thecaucus.blogs.nytimes.com/2008/01/07/civilrights/ (accessed 2/27/18).

16. Michelle Alexander, "Why Hillary Clinton Doesn't Deserve the Black Vote," *The Nation,* February 10, 2016, https://www.thenation.com/article/hillary-clinton-does-not-deserve-black-peoples-votes/ (accessed 2/27/18).

17. Yesha Callahan, "Cornel West Says Hillary Clinton is the 'Milli Vanilli of American Politics,'" *The Root,* February 24, 2016, https://thegrapevine.theroot.com/cornel-west-says-hillary-clinton-is-the-milli-vanilli-1790887942 (accessed 2/27/18).

18. W. E. B. Du Bois, "Why I Won't Vote," *The Nation,* 1956.

19. Eddie S. Glaude, Jr., and Frederick C. Harris, "The Black Vote: History Demands a Strategy for Change," *Time Magazine,* September 24, 2016, http://time.com/4504138/black-vote-blank-out/ (accessed 2/27/18).

20. Julia Ioffe, "The Believer: How Stephen Miller Went from Obscure Capitol Hill Staffer to Donald Trump's

Warm-Up Act—and Resident Ideologue," Politico.com, June 27, 2016, https://www.politico.com/magazine/sto ry/2016/06/stephen-miller-donald-trump-2016-policy -adviser-jeff-sessions-213992 (accessed 2/27/18).

The Activists 2

1. James Baldwin, *The Cross of Redemption: Uncollected Writings* (New York: Vintage, 2011), p. 114.
2. "LeBron James Has No Plans to 'Shut Up and Dribble,'" *ABC News,* February 17, 2018, http://abcnews.go.com /Sports/lebron-james-plans-shut-dribble/story?id =53169194 (accessed 2/27/18).
3. Adam Stites, "NFL Players Responded to Donald Trump with More Protests Than Ever," *SBNATION,* https:// www.sbnation.com/2017/9/24/16354916/nfl-protest-nati onal-anthem-donald-trump (accessed 2/27/18).
4. Lonnae O'Neal Parker, "In Trilogy with Muhammad Ali, the Words Hurt Joe Frazier Most," *The Washington Post,* November 8, 2011, https://www.washingtonpost .com/lifestyle/style/in-trilogy-with-muhammad-ali-the -words-hurt-joe-frazier-most/2011/11/08/gIQAg fUc3M_story.html?utm_term=.7b2a4d169eb2 (accessed 2/27/18).
5. Krishnadev Calamur, "Muhammad Ali and Vietnam," *The Atlantic,* June 4, 2016, https://www.theatlantic.com /news/archive/2016/06/muhammad-ali-vietnam/485717/ (accessed 2/27/18).
6. Stefan Fatsis, "No Viet Cong Ever Called Me Nig- ger," *Slate,* June 8, 2016, http://www.slate.com/articles /sports/sports_nut/2016/06/did_muhammad_ali_ever _say_no_viet_cong_ever_called_me_nigger.html (acces- sed 4/19/18).
7. Eric Macramalla, "Colin Kaepernick Is No Muham- mad Ali," *Forbes,* August 30, 2016, https://www.forbes .com/sites/ericmacramalla/2016/08/30/colin-kaeperni ck-is-no-muhammad-ali/#5830f6557a56 (accessed 2/27/ 18).
8. Eugene Wolfenstein, *The Victims of Democracy: Mal- colm X and the Black Revolution* (reprint, New York: Guilford Press, 1993).
9. David Davis, "Olympic Athletes Who Took a Stand," *Smithsonian Magazine,* August 2008, https://www .smithsonianmag.com/articles/olympic-athletes-who -took-a-stand-593920/ (accessed 2/27/18).

10. Dave Zirin, "MLK Wasn't an Athlete, but He Understood Importance of Sports," *Sports Illustrated,* January 18, 2010, https://www.si.com/more-sports/2010/01/18/mlk (accessed 2/27/18).
11. Peter Vescey, "From Jim Crow to Obama, Newcombe Has Seen It All," *New York Post,* January 20, 2009, https://nypost.com/2009/01/20/from-jim-crow-to-obama-newcombe-has-seen-it-all/ (accessed 2/27/18).
12. Mike Wise, "LeBron James Spoke of Emmett Till on the Eve of the NBA Finals," *The Undefeated,* May 31, 2017,https://theundefeated.com/features/lebron-james-racist-graffiti-emmett-till-eve-of-the-nba-finals/ (accessed 3/30/18).
13. Henry Abbot, "Lebron James' Decision: The Transcript," *ESPN,* July 9, 2010, http://www.espn.com/blog/truehoop/post/_/id/17853/lebron-james-decision-the-transcript (accessed 2/27/18).
14. Eleanor Barkhorn, "Cleveland Cavaliers Owner 'Sees LeBron as a Runaway Slave,' Says Jesse Jackson," *The Atlantic,* July 12, 2010, https://www.theatlantic.com/entertainment/archive/2010/07/cleveland-cavaliers-owner-sees-lebron-as-a-runaway-slave-says-jesse-jackson/59536/ (accessed 2/27/18).
15. Devon Ivie, "Beyoncé Hails 'Selfless' Colin Kaepernick During Muhammad Ali Legacy Award Speech," *W Magazine,* December 6, 2017, https://www.wmagazine.com/story/beyonce-colin-kaepernick-muhammad-ali-legacy-award-speech (accessed 2/27/18).
16. Scott Davis, "Pistons coach Stan Van Gundy Blasts Donald Trump as 'Brazenly Racist' and 'Misogynistic,' Says He's 'Ashamed' of People Who Voted for Him," *Business Insider,* November 9, 2016, http://www.businessinsider.com/stan-van-gundy-slams-donald-trump-2016-11 (accessed 2/27/18).
17. Jack Maloney, "Popovich on Trump, Protests: 'We still have no clue of what being born white means,'" *CBS Sports,* September 25, 2017, https://www.cbssports.com/nba/news/popovich-on-trump-protests-we-still-have-no-clue-of-what-being-born-white-means/ (accessed 2/27/18).

After the Meeting

1. John F. Kennedy Presidential Library & Museum. "University of Kansas (March 18, 1968)." Robert F. Kennedy

Speeches.http://www.jfklibrary.org/Research/Research
-Aids/Ready-Reference/RFK-Speeches/Remarks-of
-Robert-F-Kennedy-at-the-University-of-Kansas-March
-18-1968.aspx (accessed 4/3/18)
2. Arthur M. Schlesinger, Jr., *Robert Kennedy and His
    Times* (New York: Houghton Mifflin Company, 1978,
    2002), p. 875. All further quotes from this speech are
    from this page.
3. Michael Eric Dyson, *I May Not Get There With You: The
    True Martin Luther King, Jr.* (New York: Free Press,
    2001), p. 30; David Halberstam, "When 'Civil Rights and
    'Peace' Join Forces" (originally published as "The Sec-
    ond Coming of Martin Luther King" in *Harper's Maga-
    zine,* Aug. 1967), in C. Eric Lincoln, ed., *Martin Luther
    King, Jr.: A Profile* (New York: Hill and Wang, revised
    edition, 1985), p. 202.
4. Evan Thomas, *Robert Kennedy: His Life* (New York: Si-
    mon & Schuster, 2002, reprint), p. 367.

The Aquinnah Public Library
1 Church Street
Aquinnah, MA 02535

...but betwee

powerful and

disenfranchi

—Michael Eric Dyson on

James Baldwin